THE
ACCIDENTAL
MANAGER

THE UNCOMFORTABLE TRUTH
ABOUT JUNIOR FOOTBALL

SIMON COMPTON & MARK JONES

Matador
Unit E2 Airfield Business Park
Harrison Road, Market Harborough
Leicestershire LE16 7UL
Tel: 0116 279 2299
Email: books@troubador.co.uk
Web: www.troubador.co.uk/matador
Twitter: @matadorbooks

ISBN 978 1803136714

British Library Cataloguing in Publication Data.
A catalogue record for this book is available from the British Library.

Printed and bound by CPI Group (UK) Ltd, Croydon, CR0 4YY
Typeset in 11pt Minion Pro by Troubador Publishing Ltd, Leicester, UK

Matador is an imprint of Troubador Publishing Ltd

This book is dedicated to the millions of children who play our beautiful game. We hope that one day you will enjoy your football without adults trying to spoil it.

As well as to all the adults involved in junior football, who volunteer for the right reasons, supporting and developing children on and off the football pitch.

CONTENTS

ACKNOWLEDGEMENTS

We would like to thank all the players we managed in junior football. You were fantastic and now that you are young adults, I hope that you can look back on some fond memories of your junior football career.

Thank you to Ricky Modeste and Nicky Hayes for your help in writing this book.

Most of all thank you to our wonderful families in supporting us through all the years of football management. Being there the hundreds of cold Sunday mornings, putting up with the bad moods when we lost or got driven round the bend by parents and clubs. And, of course, listening to the endless fascinating dilemmas every week about what formation and tactics to use for the game on Sunday.

Eve, Stacey, Alex, Sam, Baby Girl, Connor and Madison – thank you, you are amazing.

NSPCC

We have decided to support the NSPCC with this book, through a donation from book sales to the NSPCC to support their vital work. These are their key messages.

The NSPCC was founded over 130 years ago to support children. Child abuse can take many forms including emotional, physical and sexual, or failing to meet the basic needs through neglect. We work tirelessly to prevent abuse from ever happening, protect children at risk and help those who have been abused to rebuild their lives.

We **prevent** abuse from happening through pioneering community projects and our work in schools, including our *Speak out, Stay safe* workshops, where we visit primary schools across the country to help children recognise the signs of abuse and understand where to go for help.

We **protect** children at risk with Childline and our NSPCC helpline. Many children have been the hidden victims of the pandemic and the effects are far from over. Childline is a confidential 24-hour service that gives children somewhere to turn. The NSPCC helpline is there for adults who are concerned about a child.

We **transform** society and help to rebuild the lives of children who have been abused. We deliver therapeutic services to enable children to move on from abuse, as well as provide resources and support for parents and families around caring for their children. We also campaign and lobby for governments to change laws and strive to keep children safe online through our programmes and partnerships.

If children or young people need to speak to someone, you can call Childline, which is a free, private and confidential service where you can talk about anything.

Call 0800 1111
Or visit www.childline.org.uk

If you have any concerns at all about child's safety or wellbeing, don't hesitate to contact our Adult Helpline. Whatever your worry we can help. We also have advice on spotting signs of abuse.

Call 0808 800 5000
Or visit www.nspcc.org.uk

FOREWORD

I first met Simon in 2016 in a work capacity. I was playing for Dover Athletic at the time, and we had just been drawn against Crystal Palace in the cup.

When he found out I was a footballer and was playing a Premiership side, I think he was more excited than me! He spent the whole meeting asking me about being a footballer, who I had played for and against, and just about any other football-related question you could think of.

He told me about the football team he managed for his son and his mates. He kept asking me to come down to one of the games to meet the kids – he was not going to take no for an answer. They were in the bottom division of the local league when I first saw them, and in all honesty the standard was not brilliant, but he was so enthusiastic about the team. He was very protective of the players; they'd had a bad time at their first club, and he was determined to look out for them and make sure they improved and enjoyed their football.

I kept in touch with the team, did a couple of end-of-season presentations and was impressed with how the team improved and developed. I thought the professional game was ruthless and political – it has nothing on the junior game! But despite the stresses and politics he always put the kids first: taking them on tour to Holland, making them ball boys and mascots at professional matches, organising social events and taking them to Billericay, Southend and West Ham games. I know he paid personally for football kits, boots, subs and tours for kids who were struggling over the years.

In the last season they had grown to the point that a second team was set up and they went on to win trophies and play in cup finals; they improved so much and did great.

I met Mark more recently and could see the same passion for junior football. This book is important to them as they want to raise awareness of the problems in junior football and, having experienced it directly for years, want it to be a better place for children. There are too many clueless adults spoiling it for kids. It has always been the same, but hopefully this could help be the start of change.

Ricky Modeste
Professional and International Footballer

TITLE DECIDER

AT A FOOTBALL PITCH SOMEWHERE IN ESSEX – MARCH 2017

We had played so well all season, we deserved to win this title. We had won fourteen league games out of fifteen – with one draw, where we were cheated out of the win by the same team we played that day. Any other season we would have won the league by now with a game or two to spare, but our opponents were also unbeaten. It was our last game; they still had two games to play, but I was in no doubt if they had beaten us, they would have easily won their last two games and won the league – we were the two best teams.

I had only set the team up at the start of the season – whatever happened, it had been a good first season, but I would never have been able to see it that way: those next seventy minutes were everything, the difference between success and failure. Nine months of work all coming down to one game of football – effectively a cup final. I felt physically sick; my stomach was doing somersaults; the fear of losing was overwhelming; I had been up since 6am, hardly slept, did four miles on the treadmill to try and calm down but still felt seriously nervous. At least it wasn't raining or too hot or cold; in fact, it was perfect football conditions. I put on a massive effort to hold it together, to appear calm in front of the boys and to give my final team talk before kick-off.

To be honest I cannot remember exactly what I said; we had spoken a lot about this match. For a few weeks we knew it was our last game; we knew that we had to keep winning to get to this position, where we could win the league on our home ground. If we drew and they won their last two games, we would have to play a playoff in a few weeks' time to decide the league – no one wanted that. One way or another, it was going to be decided today. I said something along the lines of how proud I was of them all and that if we played our game and did the things we had practised, we would win. I was terrified of their striker – he had scored fifty goals (including a hat trick when they smashed us in the cup at the start of the season). He was very good, but I also knew we had improved since then and changed our tactics to counter their big threat; it worked well in the away game in January, and I knew if we kept him quiet, we had a good chance of finally beating them. I looked around at the boys and for the first time in days I felt a little calmer; there was something in their faces which really did show me they were not losing today. Determined and focused, they had decided they were not getting to this point to be runners-up; I could just see it in their eyes.

The preparations leading up to this game had started five months previously. We had won our first few games and were looking strong; I had expected another team from a nearby town to be our rivals, but we beat them 3-0 in our first game, so already (stupidly) were thinking of winning titles but then we went up against this team in the cup. And we got smashed: their striker ran riot, we could not cope in the first half, our goalkeeper had a nightmare, we were 5-0 down at half time. Suddenly I felt very stupid indeed thinking we had the league sewn up; we had not seen this coming at all. In fairness to the boys, we regained some respectability in the second half and were much better, winning the half and losing 6-2. Out of the cup and we were in for a hell of a battle in the league. To add insult to injury a couple of their parents decided to take the piss out of our goalie during the game after he made a couple of mistakes, destroying his confidence more.

Both teams won all their league games until Christmas, and in the first week of January we played them in the coldest game I have been involved in. It was freezing, and all other games had been called off that day, but somehow our match went ahead as the pitch was just about playable with it not being completely frozen. We wanted to play it badly; training had been called off the day before and the lads came over to my house and we spoke about tactics and the game plan to ensure the cup nightmare was not repeated. They were geared up and we all wanted revenge.

We played well; first to every ball. My tactical masterplan was working: bringing our best player back to sweeper to deal with their striker and going three at the back (just call me Pep). We looked good going forward and were winning in midfield. We scored a good goal after twenty minutes, controlled the game and were looking forward to half time when they got a corner. To this day I have never seen it happen again: the corner was mishit, no height along the floor, easy to clear. But somehow the nearest defender missed it completely and our other defender, not expecting it, hit it in his own net. Gutted beyond belief – better team all half but one corner and somehow, they were even.

But the lads showed great character and took it to them again in the second half. You could see neither the players, manager nor parents could believe it was the same team they had thrashed a couple of months previously. But then, clearly not happy at being outplayed, the game degenerated into absolute chaos. The referee was a young lad, maybe fifteen, probably only a year older than the players. Every decision he made that was not for the home team was met with screams and shouts of abuse against him. The so-called 'respect barrier' had been trampled over so that some of their parents were literally on the touchline and on the pitch. My players were getting abused; the referee was terrified – he lost all control. This clearly fed through to their players and the challenges became more like assaults. It was dangerous: one of their boys jumped in two feet on our number 10, could have broken his leg – it was horrific. I will never forget one of my parents (one of the most chilled-out guys I have ever met) being incensed; I had never seen him angry.

Our big midfielder was then taken out completely, directly in front of me. The young referee went to blow his whistle, even put it to his mouth, but then heard the parents baying for blood again and decided against even giving a foul, let alone a card. He was petrified of the parents and had bottled it completely. Each foul was greeted by massive cheers from their parents; it was a bit sick to be honest. In hindsight can you blame the ref when he had a group of grown men screaming abuse? He was only a kid himself, it must have been seriously intimidating. However, it did us no favours at all because my players were getting hurt and getting no protection at all from him.

I must admit, I did not cover myself in glory by this point, making it very clear to the referee how disgusted I was. Our big midfielder got his own back on the boy that had fouled him five minutes previously. The same parents were outraged – how dare our players do anything back? And of course the referee was compliant, and our lad inexplicably got a yellow card, after at least five diabolical fouls against us being ignored. I was considering taking the team off for their own safety, when we got a corner. The ball went into the penalty box and was only half cleared to the edge of the area; our little winger had a go first time. The ball went through what seemed like a hundred players and through the mud and somehow squeezed over the goal line – it's the winner, it must be, with only five minutes left. The players on the pitch, me and the coach and subs on the side-line went crazy celebrating. Justice. After all the cheating we had still found a way to win. But wait, about twenty seconds after the goal had been awarded, the linesman, one of their parents or older brothers, put his flag up. The parents of course screamed at the referee to disallow the goal (the referee at this point had no idea why he should disallow it but knows he has to if he wants to make it to the car park after the game) and after a brief conversation with the 'linesman' the goal was disallowed because apparently the ball did not go over the goal line, despite not a single player appealing at the time.

I am not proud of how I reacted, but my players had been abused, assaulted and now this. Somehow, we got through the last five minutes and the score finished 1-1. I approached the referee after the game, let rip and their manager calmed me down. No wonder he was calm – he just got away with murder! And immediately I felt terrible, the referee had been terrified into having to cheat by a load of middle-aged men and now another middle-aged man was giving him grief. I apologised and walked back to my team and promised my players I would make the league give us a proper referee in the home match and they would be protected. Although unfair, the 1-1 score was decent; we knew then that if we won our last six games (including the home match against them) the title was ours.

We won our next five games (with a couple of scares) and guaranteed the runners-up spot with four games to spare, but the game we wanted was against our big rivals; we owed them one big time and it was winner takes all.

Preparations for the game began immediately after the away game; I made an official complaint to the league and an urgent request that we get an experienced adult referee for the return match – which we also knew was likely to be for the league, so a really big game. I was told they would 'do what they could but could not guarantee it', which was astonishing and entirely indictive of every dealing I ever had with them. I was telling them that the boys would get hurt and abused unless there was a proper referee, and their response was 'we will see what we can do'. It was also the league decider; it had to have a proper referee. Not for the first time, I started having serious doubts around the child welfare approach taken by the league. I was told to make the request again the week before the game, which of course I did. Incredibly they still would not grant my request, and in the end, I was advised to move the kick-off time to early afternoon to increase the chances of getting the strong referee needed, which I also did.

With three days to go and with me emailing regularly, highlighting the clear child welfare risks and pointing out how the league would look if they ignored my requests and a kid got seriously hurt or a riot broke out, they finally relented and allocated a senior referee experienced in adult games and older age groups. I called the referee that night and he instantly reassured me. Strong, calm and very experienced at higher levels and age groups, he was not taking shit from anyone. Huge relief all round; we now knew we would get a fair game and it was back in our hands. At least now, win or lose, it would be decided by football.

The second part of preparations was dealing with their parents and the volume of abuse we had experienced in both previous games. In the week or two before the game we must have asked half of the town to come down to support us. Mark, who managed a team in our previous club who played in the premiership, came down with most of his players and other parents. All my players' families, other local parents and kids, anyone I could think of. I also made sure that our parents and fans were on the half of the pitch where our linesman would be as I did not want the lad who did the line for us to have the inevitable abuse if he did the line in that half.

The final part of the preparations was to put the spectator

barrier up twice the normal distance. In the last game it had been ignored and the parents had pushed the rope forward until they were on the pitch. We put it far enough away that they would have to knock down the actual poles if they did it again – which would mean the match would be stopped and it put up again.

With fifteen minutes to go, to my disappointment we just seemed to have our usual parents in attendance – and our opponents had about the same. Suddenly everyone seemed to arrive and as we did our final team talk, we had a great crowd and completely outnumbered their parents and fans. It was all set up, we had done everything right in preparation, everyone else had done their bit by coming, half the battle was over – now the boys just had to win the game.

Looking back, it is all a blur. I remember we started off well; our specialist sweeper for the game dealt with their dangerman very well in the first ten minutes a couple of times. We were the better team but without many actual chances. It was loud and intense but not too much great football, as is often the way in cup finals; it was so nerve-wracking. Still 0-0 at half time, we urged the boys to keep going and to try and pass it a bit more and the goal would come. The second half started much the same and then, about ten minutes in, the ball was bouncing around somewhere just inside their half slightly to the left. Our goal-scoring midfielder number 4 was first to the ball and, without hesitating or even thinking about it, took a swing at the bouncing ball and connected perfectly. The ball flew through the air and dipped at the right time over the keeper and under the crossbar. In the two or three seconds between the ball being kicked and it going in the net, I just remember being grabbed by my assistant and him saying, "It's going in, it's fucking going in." The next second the whole pitch had erupted: the players were going mental, we were going mental, parents were going mental. That few seconds in time could only be described as paradise, out-and-out pure joy. If you could sell that feeling you would be a billionaire.

After we all calmed down, I screamed to my captain to get them focused; we still had twenty minutes or more to play. The next fifteen minutes seemed like a lifetime; our opponents were getting desperate by then, and their manager and parents (who had been drowned out for most of the game by our fans) found their voice and started appealing for penalties, free kicks and, within a minute's period, appealed for a handball three times, none of which were even close. In an attempt to ease the situation and highlight how ridiculous it was getting, the next time one of their players controlled the ball (with their chest or even just with their foot) I screamed as loud as I could, "HANDBALL, REF." That raised a laugh and eased the tension a bit, and it worked because their manager stopped doing it, realising it was ridiculous.

With five to go, our number 10 picked up the ball wide on the left-hand side, turned the full back brilliantly, cut in and suddenly had a great chance of a shot at goal. This was it, where we would seal the league, but his shot hit the post – I felt like crying. They went up the other end and in the last minute their winger was on the right-hand side of the penalty area just outside and our full back tripped him. Free kick on the edge of the area in the last minute of normal time. This was so dangerous; from that distance if it was hit left-footed towards goal anything could happen – could go straight in or any touch and it would be in. I was sure I was about to have a heart attack. But they sent a right-footed player to take it – still dangerous but better for us. Bad decision, in my opinion, but I loved it. For what seemed an eternity the kick was lined up, the cross finally went in and, to my absolute joy (almost as much as when the goal went in), it was not a great connection and we cleared it.

We were now in injury time. I made a final sub, the ball was cleared one last time and the most wonderful sound I had ever heard came with the referee blowing for full time.

The rest really was a blur; I vaguely remember running onto the pitch, hugging all the players, hugging all the parents. Everyone was on that pitch. Some of the boys from the other team were laying down on the pitch, completely devastated. I tried to console them, which I am sure was pretty useless to them. But the one thing I clearly remember is the utter relief to have done it – joy was the few seconds when the goal went in, but this was just pure relief, relief that the boys had got what they deserved, that they had not been cheated again. They had worked so hard and came together so well as a team; it would have been a travesty if we had not won. Helping them experience that joy was just a beautiful moment for me and my assistant; we had all worked so hard. And to win that dramatically – no under-fourteen match finishes 1-0!

We had a drink at a local working man's club after the game; I had booked it on the basis that, win or lose, the boys had done well and the season deserved to be celebrated. Not sure I could have gone if we had lost, though. It was a lovely afternoon; I remember walking in with my son and all the parents and players who were already there giving us a round of applause – great memories. Another nice touch was a text from our opponent's manager congratulating us, which I read out. So much had happened that season, but in the end, it was decided the right way: both teams playing a great game and being allowed to play football without any adult nonsense.

I slept much better that night than the night before, that is for sure – helped, no doubt, by copious amounts of lager and JD.

And the greatest part of the day was that my son and his friends had experienced something special that he could look back on forever. That is what football does; it is magical, completely illogical, but in many ways truly is the beautiful game. We play it, we watch it, we talk about it for hours and weeks and months and years of our lives. Those rare moments when it goes perfectly, you remember forever. It is like a drug; there is no sense to it, completely illogical yet addictive and capable of giving you the highest highs and lowest lows.

But that day and that game was not at Upton Park (or rather the London Stadium) or any other professional club with a proper stadium. It was on a field in Essex, on a pitch that we had to mark out and with goals with nets that we had to put up, with numerous holes in.

It was not for the Premiership title or any professional title; it was also not for the Sunday league premiership title. It was the sixth division of the local league, the bottom division of that league, probably the lowest standard of any form of league football in the country. Yet to me, the players and many parents, it was for the Premiership title and World Cup rolled into one, and when our number 4 scored that thirty-five-yarder to win the game (which to this day I know he meant, whatever his teammates say), I had not felt that good since Marlon Harewood scored the winner for West Ham in the 2006 FA Cup Semi Final, eleven years previously. There must have been 150 spectators that day, the most I have ever seen for a junior football league match. Not bad for a division six game. Some semi-professional teams don't get many more fans on a cold evening kick-off. Again, it shows the power and passion of football; it was a big day for everyone. There were tears from players and parents. It was dramatic, emotional and wonderful.

I know it is sad, I admit it. I have a wife, three kids and run a business. League decider or not, a game of junior football SHOULD NOT MEAN THAT MUCH! But with football it's either in you or not. You still feel the same passion as you did going to your first game as a child on days like that. And that day in March 2017 was the perfect example of why we love it so much. The level and division were irrelevant; it meant the world to everyone involved and the boys created their own little piece of history that day.

SC

INTRODUCTION

My last game as a junior football manager was at Roots Hall, the home of Southend United, in the Under 16 League Cup Final for the local junior league. As a junior team, to play in a cup final at a professional ground, with changing rooms, dug-outs, seats and terraces as well as a proper referee and two linesmen, is the ultimate experience; it does not get bigger. Like my first game as a manager over five years previously, we lost, but we had come a long way in that time. It had been a crazy but wonderful season; we had already won our division and another cup. Just getting to Roots Hall and being able to pretend to be a professional team for the day was a fantastic achievement. We also went to Holland on tour a few weeks later, after the boys had finished their GCSEs – more fantastic memories. It was the perfect end to the madness of junior football management.

When I took on the role of my son's football team's manager at the under-twelve age group all I really wanted was for him and his mates to make friendships, to enjoy being part of a team and, of course, to enjoy football, to improve and hopefully experience winning a trophy or getting to a cup final. I still have my own memories of playing in a cup final at a similar age and level and winning sometime in the late 1980s. If you have the football bug, and millions of us do, football memories stay with you forever and the level or age is irrelevant. Any cup final might as well be the World Cup Final; the level of passion and excitement is exactly the same when you are part of it.

It sounds straightforward. After all, surely all the adults involved in junior football, the parents, leagues and clubs, want these same positive experiences for our children. Think again: the kids are the easy part. I was incredibly fortunate and very rarely had any issues with players; they were all brilliant. The parents, clubs and leagues, not easy at all.

There is much truth in Bill Shankly's quote: "Football is a simple game, complicated by idiots." At professional level I am sure most football fans would agree with this. Even in recent years I look at the absolute mess made of VAR, which could have improved the game, or the bungled 'Super League' farce, or the repeated failures to deal with racism internationally. Not to mention the absolutely appallingly corrupt and immoral decision to host the last World Cup in a country with an appalling human rights record in stadiums built using slave labour with many workers dying whilst building the very stadiums we will all watch our next fix of football. At junior football level there are different problems. I would change the great man's quote slightly to: "Junior football is a simple game, complicated and often ruined by adults." Throughout this book the biggest recurring theme is the curse of middle-aged men that should know better; it comes up time and time again.

Parents have an enormous impact on junior football; their behaviour will always determine how a match is going to play out, how abusive and aggressive the game will be on and off the pitch, more so than the managers and the players. As with anything in life, some parents are great, but a sizeable minority cause major problems for everyone involved.

After two Covid-interrupted, unfinished seasons since my last season, I went to watch an under-sixteen game between two local teams. It had been three years since I had managed a team, but nothing had changed at all – if anything, it was worse. It was an end-of-season meaningless game between two mid-table teams in the lower divisions of the local junior league. A group of dads had mistaken this game for some sort of war. Dad 1 spent most of the game screaming criticism to his own son: "You are fucking out of position again," "You're too quiet," "For fuck's sake, put a challenge in."

Dad 2 was more focused on all the midfielders rather than his own son: "Midfield, you are a fucking disgrace," "There is only one player on the pitch who wants it," and, of course, the classic: "They don't want it," referring to a young lad playing for the other side barely five yards away.

For some reason, the home team had not put the 'respect barrier' up, probably thinking they could trust the parents to give the boys some space as it was in theory a fairly insignificant game, unlikely to provoke too much emotion. Big mistake: the three dads thought it acceptable to stand on the touchline completely blocking the view of the linesman as well as obstructing the actual players. At one point the ball rolled towards them, chased by one of their own players trying to keep it in. Dad 3 actually kept the ball in, entering the pitch, which the three of them found hilarious. The boy chasing the ball was understandably fuming; he just wanted to play a game of football and have space on the pitch to keep the ball in without being impeded by idiot adults. The referee stopped the game and, I thought, was coming over to tell the dads to back up and let the boys play or tell the home team to put up the spectator barrier. Sadly, he did nothing, clearly intimidated by the three stooges.

A minute later, Dad 1 really excelled himself, taking a more 'retro' approach with his insults, telling one of his players who had mis-controlled and lost the ball that he had 'the first touch of a rapist', once again invoking laughter between the three of them. No one said a thing, no one did a thing, me included. I had no involvement in either team, just watching a game of football, and I didn't really fancy a row on a Sunday morning, which is a pathetic excuse. Clearly the referee, manager and other parents were also wary of intervening, though, and there lies the problem. Nice positive messages on a website and clubs telling themselves how they will not tolerate abusive behaviour is great until they actually see abusive behaviour and don't fancy going up against three charmers like this.

I had seen many similar situations when I was managing (thankfully never from my own parents – where I would have intervened); it was just depressing that another three years had gone by and nothing had changed or improved at all. Now I am not involved personally, I can look at things objectively and admit that this is not right. Adults should not be behaving so badly in front of children. I love football, but

I cannot defend the indefensible. The level of aggression and language is unacceptable; it would not be legal or accepted on the street. I would get arrested if I started screaming abuse at an adult, let alone a child. Why is this allowed on a Sunday morning if it is around a football pitch? It is not 'passion' or 'part of the game'; it is completely wrong.

I never understand the anger a parent must have inside them to start behaving in such a disgusting way in front of children. Perhaps football is just another reason to get angry in an increasingly unstable and emotional society, but then it has always been the same irrespective of other wider factors. Where football is so emotional, all logic and intelligence is ignored most of the time. When we watch our team, the identical tackle made by our team's centre back is fair and the striker is a 'cheating diving cunt'. When it is done by the opposition's centre back on our striker, it is a 'stonewall' penalty, the centre back should be sent off and the 'referee is a wanker'. Where emotion trumps logic and facts, reactions and behaviours do become unpredictable; we see this all the time when supporting our professional teams. But these wild emotions and behaviours are also displayed on a Sunday morning all over the country whilst children just want to have a game of football.

I have seen parents screaming at their own players to 'take out' my players. I have seen parents tell my players to 'fuck off'. I have seen parents screaming out to eleven-year-old kids that 'he don't want it' to put them off their game. I have seen parents scream out on a weekly basis abusing referees and linesmen (who are just parents who had the decency to not run away when the flag came out), anything from 'fuck off, lino' through to 'ref, you're a cunt', all in front of children. I have seen young referees intimidated to the point that they are petrified to give any decisions to the other team because they have been threatened. I have seen managers screaming abuse at officials, literally frothing at the mouth, and telling us we are 'fucking cheats'. The list goes on and on; this is happening every week all over the country. It is absolutely no surprise that the players for the teams with the most horrible parents are the most aggressive and violent players. If a child has seen their own dad calling the referee a 'fucking wanker' they probably won't end up having much respect for referees themselves.

Ironically when you look at the professional game the players are better behaved than ever before. The England players are absolute role models. Talented, hard-working, articulate young men; they really are everything good about the game and society. We all love the characters from the old days of football pre-Premiership, but this new generation really are fantastic role models for our children.

Equally, at the time of writing the England women's team have recently won the Euros. They were absolutely fantastic and not only played brilliantly with fantastic ability and determination but the positive way they conducted themselves was wonderful to see. No diving, tantrums or abuse of officials. The fans as well – completely different to the men's game. No violence and toxic masculinity bullshit; it was actually all about the beautiful game, very refreshing. Clearly the common denominator on and off the pitch is men, which is very worrying, and grassroots football (still predominantly a male environment) is a million miles away from the millionaires of the Premiership. Children internalise and copy their parents or manager's behaviour, not the brilliant footballers we watch on TV.

When you are managing a junior team, 75% of the role is an absolute ball-ache; for every good day, you have to go through far more bad days. But when it does work and you do achieve something special – whether it be winning a game for the first time, managing to get all the team away on tour (which is more difficult than winning the treble when it means getting sixteen parents' agreement on dates and, importantly, sixteen payments) or playing in a cup final – it is worth it. All the time you spent in the freezing cold and pouring rain becomes worth it. Every moan and insult you had to put up with from ungrateful parents and every idiot you had to contend with from the club and league becomes worth it. All the abuse and at times actual violence you had to witness and experience against managers, other parents, officials – it is still worth it. But when you are out of it and can witness games and the workings of junior football more objectively and with far less crazy emotions, you start thinking rationally as a parent and responsible adult, and realise that no one should have to put up with any of it. Not the managers, not the referees and most of all not the children. None of this should be accepted as 'normal' or 'part of the game'.

Leagues and officials do not always help the situation. I have seen many referees cheat and give constant decisions to their preferred team (mates with the manager or scared of his parents). Being a linesman is the worst job in the world and any parent who steps up will almost certainly be abused for ninety minutes, but some do cheat and will do anything for their team to win, which, of course, is guaranteed to cause huge upset.

As with the professional game, the local leagues and clubs seem completely removed from what goes on every weekend. They talk a great game and have wonderful websites and social media messaging with hundreds of positive messages referring to 'respect', 'fair play', 'equality', 'anti-racism' and numerous other buzzwords. But they are just words, soundbites, which are not backed up by actions. Go to any match on a Sunday morning and it will be a miracle if all of these messages are demonstrated, or even some of them. Punishments for any of these offences are pointless or non-existent, and with no deterrent it will carry on. I have repeatedly seen the most 'vocal' clubs talk fantastic games, but when there is actual trouble and violent incidents they are nowhere to be seen. There are hundreds of cases of children and referees being abused physically and verbally from 'parents' every week.

The politics within the leagues and clubs is soul-destroying; the frustration managers have in trying to get anything done is huge. The levels of incompetence and at times even corruption is staggering. When everyone is a 'volunteer' it is impossible to criticise or even question anything at all, so of course nothing changes. I am sure most adults going into junior football have good intentions and genuinely want to put the children's interests first when volunteering to take on any role within a league or club, but you do get quite a few who are more interested in a little power and their own ego, and the children's welfare gets forgotten.

I lost count of the times I was told, "You can do my job if you don't like how I am doing it," when raising a perfectly reasonable concern or suggestion about child welfare. That is not a reasonable answer in any walk of life if a parent or coach is raising perfectly legitimate concerns – volunteer or no volunteer.

Just as there is not a 'right way' to play football, there is not a 'right way' to manage. Success can be measured in many ways; for me the greatest success was creating an environment where the boys were happy and lasting friendships were formed. In an environment where teams around us were folding every season, we rarely had a player want to leave and many wanted to join, which was more important than any trophy. Even in the early days when we were losing every game and having a horrible time of it with the club, boys were still very loyal and kept coming back, which to me was the greatest achievement.

On the pitch, I always believed that the only meaningful measure of success was to improve. Whether that is improving to the point of winning trophies or just to win a single game in a season, I have been in both positions, and seeing a team grow and helping children play to the best of their ability is definitely one of the positives that makes up for all the negatives. For Mark and myself, we were not remotely interested in what clubs, leagues or even parents to a large extent thought of us as managers. The only people that matter are the players who played for us; they are all young men now and I would like to think that the vast majority look back fondly on some great experiences and know that we always tried to look out for them.

There really is not a 'right' or 'wrong' way; all children are different and obviously they change every year, especially as they become young men and women. One size does not fit all, which is something I always found the clubs could not grasp. An under-sixteen team is a different world to an under-twelve team; the same way of managing these teams won't work. Discussion and different views are healthy and should be encouraged, not shut down. In my experience, there seems to be many adults within leagues and clubs, who don't even like football half the time, telling everyone how children feel and what they want, rather than actually speaking to them and finding out how they feel.

Another annoyance we had to endure was other managers of local teams trying to 'tap up' our players. This was not the Premiership; we did not have agents and transfer fees. Why unsettle a perfectly happy child who is enjoying his football? At that age children are impressionable, and the empty promises of 'glory' will get to them. Time after time I would hear that another team wanted our best players; it was so tedious. We even arranged friendly matches once or twice purely to beat the teams trying it on to ensure players had no reason to leave; it was ridiculous.

Despite all the negatives, football is still the beautiful game. No other sport can provoke the same emotions and drama felt by billions of peoples all over the world. The first reference point in millions of first conversations when two blokes meet is what team they both support. It really is a worldwide language and if the huge emotions it provokes are channelled well it is truly beautiful and can bring people together. Junior football is no different; we had some brilliant times and the bonus of watching children grow into brilliant young adults was an absolute privilege. My son is still close friends with many of the players; some have become close family friends. I am good mates with many of the parents and the boys are now at an age where they can take us old gits out for a pint! That is what football should be about: good times and friendships.

But things really should change. Our children deserve a chance to enjoy their football free from any abuse and without it being spoilt by adults. If nothing changes, we are going to carry on taking our children to football and putting up with the nonsense because we all love football. But that is not a reason to do nothing; the junior football experience could be so much better. We all know what the problems are, the same as thirty years ago when I was playing junior football. There is no simple answer, but that should not mean we give up and accept it will never change. It is damaging our children and sets a terrible example which will only pass the same attitudes and behaviours on to them as they become adults. In my last season at under-sixteens, most games were like the wild west; these 'children' were now young adults, many of them were well on the way to becoming their parents. But if they had experienced positive behaviour from the adults around them since childhood at their games it would all be so different.

I first met Mark when my son wanted to play football for one of our local teams (called United in this book) when he was eleven. Mark had set up the original team in the age group a few years previously and they had expanded to the point that there were enough boys for three teams. I could see immediately how passionate he was about junior football and helping the kids. My son had never really played before, but he could not have been more welcoming, inviting us down to the next training session. I sometimes wish he had not been so welcoming, as this interaction started a five-year journey into junior football, most of which was complete aggravation! But at the same time, it started a very special journey which gave great experiences to many children and formed friendships both between the children and their parents which are still going strong now. So, all things considered I am pleased he invited us to training all those years ago.

Mark became a real mentor to me; he had his own team (the top team who were very good), but he still always had time for me to give advice and help, which in the early days particularly was pretty much every week. He genuinely did care for the children's welfare and really did look out for his players and cared about all players across the age group. We did not always agree on everything but neither of us held it against each other; we knew that fundamentally we had similar beliefs and outlooks. Even when the club was behaving very badly, often completely forgetting or ignoring child welfare, and we were effectively forced to change clubs, we always got on well and he was always supportive, the only one that was. Ironically, he ended up taking his team to another club too the season after us; the club really did not cover themselves with glory when it came to our age group.

Mark's team always played at a higher level to our team; in the top division of the league, the premiership. Obviously, his players were better, and the game was quicker, but the more interesting observation when I watched a few of his games was how more aggressive and volatile it was on and off the pitch with parents. By under-sixteen it had levelled up, and all parents and games were horrible, but in the younger age groups, I realised I was having an easy ride compared to that. I remember going to an under-fourteen game to watch his team play; it was like World War 3. Parents wanted to fight his parents and even him in the car park. Parents screaming, their manager screaming – it was awful.

This observation is borne out in Mark's experiences with parents, which are generally worse than I had to deal with, some of which he writes about. There just seemed to be more aggression, and everything far more toxic and frenzied. Possibly parents thinking that as they were in the top division, their son had a chance to 'make it' and so more depended on every game – who knows? It makes no sense still as even the premiership of our local league is multiple levels away from anything close to the pro ranks. But since when did parents show any logic or common sense!

Mark stepped back from managing his team in my second-to-last season for reasons he will go into. Near the end of my last season, we were doing well and had improved so much that we were ready to go into the premiership at under-seventeen level and take on his old team. Having been out of the game for a year, I thought he might be tempted to take my team over and challenge his old team. He wisely declined this dubious 'opportunity', but I hope he took it as a compliment as he was the only guy I trusted to look out for my players who I had watched grow up since kids. We had done really well and had an opportunity to play in the same top division he had always managed; I was sure my team would have had a great chance of winning the premiership with him, but it wasn't to be. It did not really matter as politics raised its ugly head again and the boys were not even allowed to move to the top division despite thoroughly deserving to. And then Covid wrote the season off before it ended.

This book is split between my personal journey covering the five seasons I managed my team from under-twelves to under-sixteens and the much bigger issues all junior managers face. Between us I hope we can provide an insight into the reality of junior football, and you never know, someone somewhere with some authority might realise it needs to change. I really wanted Mark to be involved in tackling these subjects and sharing some of his experiences and was delighted when he agreed to co-write it, which we have done in several chapters. In some areas we have very similar experiences and views and have jointly written the chapter, whilst in one or two we have different opinions and have written separately about our experiences and viewpoints. We seem to be quite unusual within junior football in that we can hold different opinions and have disagreements whilst respecting the other's position.

The one thing we both kept coming back to in our early discussions was that so much that goes on in junior football is wrong. At the time we were very emotionally involved and tolerated and accepted the behaviours we all know are wrong. After all, it is football, we love it and we have to put up with all the madness. Our children had to see too much bad behaviour from adults; it would be nice to think it could get better for the next generation. Neither of us hold out too much hope. You will see a lot of references to the lads and the boys; this is purely because neither of us ever managed a girls' team. It is wonderful to see more girls coming into football inspired by the fantastic women's international team.

We have both spoken to hundreds of parents, club officials and other managers over the years. Nothing we have said will be disputed by anyone involved in junior football. Universally it is accepted that the behaviour going on every Sunday is completely unacceptable. There are no arguments: everyone agrees. Whatever has been done to date has not worked, so it must be time for a more purposeful approach with far more actual action. Our experiences with the county FA, local leagues and club were also far from unique to us. Most managers I spoke to hated dealing with the tiresome politics and bureaucracy when dealing with leagues and clubs.

This book is an account of some of our experiences in junior football. The good times, bad times, sad times and funny times. We have changed teams and people's names to protect identities. I am sure some people would disagree with our views, but that is fine; football and everything surrounding it polarises views like nothing else. Facts cannot be disputed though, and where we have included quotes, we have all the communications and can prove anything stated. Similarly, the matches and achievements quoted are entirely correct and have been officially recorded by the leagues we played in.

I was so lucky in my experiences as a junior football manager. Although the majority of time it was not much fun, I had so many good people around me, it was all worth it when I look back at the experiences we all had. The players were sensational, and my parents were generally great. I used to look at the parents of the other team and realise just how lucky I was. The parents in my last season were so important to the team and their support was brilliant (from most of them, at least!). I also want to thank my younger son, who missed me having much involvement in his junior football career but was always so supportive. And, of course, my wife, who kicked every ball in every game with me and put up with the fascinating discussions in the week leading up to a game, debating whether to go three or four at the back. She was amazing; I could not have done it or kept my sanity without her.

Being a junior football manager is an emotional roller coaster. You have the highest highs and lowest lows. The actual football is only a small part of the job; the hard part happens off the pitch. You end up being a teacher, parent, taxi driver and social worker all rolled into one. You have to put up with alarming levels of bullshit from all quarters, and often see and experience things that you would rather not have seen. You see children brought up and treated in ways you fundamentally disagree with; it can be very upsetting. But with football, if it is in your blood, you keep going despite the insanity going on around you and because you don't want to let the kids down. In the same way I have not seen my team West Ham win a trophy since I was six years old, you keep going back despite it all. Mark is a Liverpool fan, at least his team wins things; I have no logical reason to keep going back! But then football is anything but logical.

SC

I got into youth football because my son wanted to join a team and loved playing from a very young age; I never pressured him into playing but he was never without a ball from pretty much his first steps. The game was just natural to him, so I took him along to the local club's 'little kickers' when he was six and that was where it all started. I was thirty-two at the time and only played pub football but enjoyed everything about it. I wasn't the fittest player on the pitch and was getting injured quite a lot, so it was time to hang up my boots, but I still needed my fix.

After a few weeks of my son playing, I approached the guy who was taking the team on as I had heard he would need some help. That was when I put myself forward, letting him know I would help him out, putting the cones out and collecting balls. I had no intention of getting heavily involved because at the time I worked a lot of weekends and could not be fully committed, but once I started helping out – I was hooked, and it wasn't long before I started running the training sessions and then taking the team over completely.

The first few years were great fun, and on the pitch we were improving as a team and as individuals, which was always my goal. Our best seasons would be winning Division 1 and going up to the premier division in our local league and then a couple of seasons later finishing third in the premier league. However, it was not always plain sailing off the pitch, as, unlike Simon, my last game wasn't covered in glory. In the season I quit as manager I actually wanted to stop before the season started but was talked into giving it one more season by my coach. I had already started to ask another dad to help out in training so the lads could get used to him and I knew my coach was more than capable of taking over the team.

I didn't realise it at the time, but I was well on my way to having a mental breakdown, having started a house renovation whilst running my own business along with managing my son's football team which I had managed for eight years. It is stressful enough running a junior football team and dealing with parents, club officials and leagues. Combined with other areas of life not running smoothly, it does become very stressful, and the football is very time-consuming. It was beginning to take its toll on my mental health.

We also had to contend with a problem parent who had taken a jealous dislike to my wife and proceeded to abuse her to anyone that would listen and try to turn the other parents against her. Needless to say, the other parents and people around us could see exactly what she was trying to do and that she had a history of falling out with other people. Nevertheless, after a year of shit from a jealous, small-minded parent, it started to take its toll.

In my last game I don't really remember much apart from shouting at one of the lads to get off the pitch as he was questioning our line-up and formation for the game. Had the team got on with their usual game we would have rolled over this team with ease. Having had a go at the boy, I then proceeded to walk around the pitch to tell his dad (who was doing the line) to take his lad home and to give me the flag. More heated words were exchanged at half time, and I said that was it for me to my coach and kept out of the way. After the match I thanked the lads and said I was done. Not the best way or right way to quit. Some of the parents sent some lovely messages and, once some other teams had heard what had happened, some other managers even text me, which was very kind.

So that was it: after eight and a half years my time was up. I threw everything I had at it, but as mentioned earlier, it was contributing badly to my mental health. Saying that, I made some of the best memories of my life, met some fantastic people along the way and some I still call my friends. Like most managers, they need help (although very rarely get it from most parents) and we had the best in someone who became known as my football wife (nicknamed by my wife). She was the most fantastic woman you could have ever met; in fact, her whole family were brilliant. Her husband and their three kids – without her our life would have been that bit more difficult. My wife and my football wife would arrange the Christmas party, making sure all the players and their siblings got a gift. They would help out organising the presentation along with any other events and I can tell you, the effort put into these events was immense and I will be forever grateful. It's these people who make a team work and without them the cogs wouldn't turn so easily. So, thank you.

The days out watching Southend United and when we were kindly invited to be ball boys for the match, the tournament at Charlton Athletic's stadium was described by one of the lads as the best day of his life so far are memories that will stay with me forever, but the things that really counted for me were seeing the kids with smiles on their faces in training and the kids' progress over the years – that, for me, is what it was really all about. It is impossible to keep everyone happy all the time, but I knew the majority were most of the time.

I am sure my son, like most other managers' sons, bore the brunt of bad performances, but that's not intentional. I just hope as he gets older he appreciates what I was trying to do and what I took on as a football coach. I mean, we all take it for granted until we actually get up and do it. I contacted one of my old managers who now lives in Germany to thank him for the role he played in my life as a football manager; I wasn't the easiest kid to manage, but he always kept calm and it was only when I started managing my son's team that I really appreciated the work he put in. Most of the role is a thankless task, but the experiences in working with the lads and seeing the improvement and development on and off the pitch makes it all worthwhile. But it is about getting the balance right, which, as I found out, was hard to do. I have to say, I respect every man or woman who puts themselves forward to manage or coach a team; it would just be appreciated if every parent could do the same.

Running a team affects your whole family: my wife constantly had to listen to me going on about football almost every day – the highs, the lows and everything else in between – but she always stood by me and by my decisions; my poor daughter, getting dragged along to matches week in week out in all weathers, sometimes with other siblings to play with and sometimes sitting in a chair bored until the final whistle. Without them and their support it would have made things a hell of a lot harder; I'm a very lucky man to have the family I have.

MJ

THE GOOD

The best part of being a junior football manager is working with the kids. More accurately, the only good part of being a junior football manager is working with the kids, and they make all the other rubbish worthwhile.

We have written separate accounts of our experiences in this area. We had different teams, players and experiences. We do, however, both categorically agree that this really was the good part of being a junior football manager. We saw some superb wording on a Twitter post recently which to us really summed up everything important about being a junior football manager. Of course, the winning is brilliant, and winning trophies and playing in cup finals is even better. But the greatest achievement is making a positive difference to a young life. Ultimately the football does not matter, which is something sadly missed by many adults involved in grassroots football.

In grassroots football the coach's true legacy is having a positive impact on young players' lives; the greatest achievement is not changing a game but helping to change a life. This is worth more than any medal or cup.

MJ & SC

There are many pros and cons to being a manager, coach or even just being involved in helping run a grassroots football team, you meet some fantastic people and some not-so-fantastic people along the way, and I am lucky enough to have walked away from managing a team having made some really good friends, But fundamentally for me it was all about the lads improving as players and enjoying the game along with trying to win some trophies along the way. If we are truly honest, no matter what level you play at, you will always want to win. I heard an old coach once say, "It's just as hard to win division five as it is to win the premier league," so nothing should be taken away from the achievement no matter what level it is.

The good times were really good, and when I say good times it's parents and players enjoying themselves, as both come hand in hand. One season we won the first division having finished fifth the season before; everything clicked. I always encouraged the team to pass it around and play good football as we were not the biggest team but technically had some brilliant players. In one game the opposing parents likened the team to being like watching Barcelona! Obviously as a coach it is great to hear and a confidence boost for the players and myself, as a coach proving that things are working and the lads are progressing not only as individuals but also as a team.

I loved that year winning the first division; after all,

everyone loves some silverware at the end of a season. But my favourite season was our first season at eleven-a-side at under-thirteens. We were now playing in our local premier league, but the season before we had lost our star player to a junior alliance team and ended up finishing second from bottom. Normally it would have seen us automatically relegated back to the first division, but because we were going from nine-a-side up to eleven-a-side we could have a choice and we would have to get some more players in. I was sure we would be asking to play back in the first division to help us be competitive. But on our final game of the season, we played the premier league winners. I was expecting a thumping; this team was brilliant, the best in the county, and proved it by winning the county cup on more than one occasion. Their manager was ruthless, a top bloke but a winner, and so was his team; he now manages at National League South level. We walked away from the game losing 2-0, with the second goal being scored in the last minute of the match. I had seen enough spirit and commitment from the lads that day to tell me to keep them playing in the premier league; I just had to grow their confidence, as the ability and effort was there.

The first eleven-a-side season we attracted some good players to add to the squad. Along came a brilliant goalkeeper, a couple of midfielders, a striker and a centre back, making us a squad of fourteen, which was perfect at eleven-a-side. We gelled in our preseason friendlies and went into the season feeling confident and looking a strong team. Just before the start of our last preseason friendly, as I walked over to the pitch one of the players' dads approached me and asked for a quick word. Disaster struck when he proceeded to tell me his son was leaving to go and play for another team. At first, I was in total shock, but if any player was going to leave it would have been him. He lived in the next town along from ours and had played for the team a good few years. When he turned up, he had been playing left back, but with his pace, power and wand of a left foot I moved him to left wing, where he developed his game hugely. He was a great player but an even greater lad: always worked hard, got on well with everyone and would ask the most random questions which made me laugh at times. He wanted to go and play in the same team that his mates played for. I was gutted but got it; they were a better team than us and played in the same division. I always said to the lads that if they had a chance to play at a higher level, they should take it.

In the last friendly game, the lads knew he would be leaving before the match; he was really nervous at the reaction from them, but I think they got it. They even let him take a penalty in the game which he would not have taken in normal circumstances, but I thought it was a nice touch from the lads. At the end of the match, he shook hands and hugged the lads before thanking myself and the coach for everything we had done for him. I wished him all the best and said if he ends up playing on TV don't forget me! I walked over to his parents after the game to thank them for their support over the years and let them know I would need his kit back as it was club rules, which they were fine with. I didn't actually need the kit as our new one was arriving in the week ready for our first game of the season. When I got the kit back from the parents, I took the shirt to training and asked the lads to sign it and put a little message on it to wish him luck. Without any hesitation they all did it, which showed the respect they had for the lad even though they were gutted he was leaving.

I dropped the shirt back at his house one evening but he wasn't in so I gave it to his mum, who was a bit emotional and said she would miss our team's parents also. Later that evening I got a lovely text from the lad from his mum's phone, which put a smile on my face and again I wished him all the best for the coming season.

So, we ended up starting the season with a squad of thirteen, which wasn't ideal; I had lost my left-winger and needed to replace him, so it was an obvious choice for us to pick the only other left-footed player to fill the position. I wouldn't say he or his parents were overly happy to move him from central midfield to left wing, but again it showed what a great lad had joined us, as he just got on with the task in hand. We were a team who got the ball out to both our wingers as much as possible as they offered great quality from those areas, and it showed with the new left-winger contributing with fifteen goals that season.

We were in a very tough league with the top two teams playing each other in the county cup final, so finishing third that season behind those teams was a great achievement for the lads. To go from finishing second from bottom to third in the local premier league and competing with the best two teams in the county showed how far we had come as a team. I was very proud of them; we played some great football along the way, winning some tight games, but seeing the togetherness of the squad and the parents was something extra special and it was my favourite season as their manager.

The lads always loved a tournament and so did the parents, although some wouldn't admit it. We used to try and enter three tournaments in the summer months if we could, playing in some tough ones, meeting some good people. We even met Rod Stewart at one and he was kind enough to have some pics taken with some of the lads. I am not sure the kids were that impressed as they probably didn't know who Rod Stewart was, but myself and the parents certainly were. We used to do pretty well in these tournaments, which always made it a better day out, but winning our first one at under-nines was brilliant. We turned up with what I thought was a decent little team, but you never know who you will be playing in your group until you turn up, so it's a bit of a lottery. The group we ended up in was pretty even; I would say we all could have beaten each other on the day, but we ended up getting through to the knockout stages.

When we turned up the weather was OK, but as the day went on the heavens opened and the rain absolutely poured down. Although we had a gazebo to stand under, the boys all got soaked, which was not good, but the weather didn't dampen (excuse the pun) the day. This was a big tournament with all age groups, so after the big downpour and well on our way to the final, a manager from our club, but a couple of age groups above, spotted us and could see how soaked the lads were. He approached me and said he had some spare shirts in his kit bag and that we could borrow them as they were dry. I jumped at the chance to at least get the lads in a dry shirt; the only problem was the size of the shirts. The team was a couple of years older so the shirts swamped most of the boys, who had to tuck them into their shorts and roll the sleeves up. Nevertheless, they were dry tops!

The lads went on to win the tournament and they were presented with a large cup, which we were allowed to keep, and individual medals. Our captain at the time couldn't wait to get his hands on the cup and lifted it like it was the World Cup, running out of the room where it was presented onto the field like the 1966 England team. It was brilliant as the players passed it around, drinking what was probably Pepsi or another soft drink out of it. Those are some of the memories that will stick with me forever and I hope the lads will remember that day, as it was special, not just because of the winning but because of the smiles on everyone's faces. I still to this day have the team photo with them holding the cup and their oversized shirts on up on my office wall at home some ten years later.

Another great day was playing in a tournament at Charlton Athletic's stadium. We arranged for a bus to take us and bring us home; the boys got to go into the changing rooms and have a little look around, some jumping in the empty bath, pretending to be a pro player after a match. I remember one of the lads jokingly standing next to the whiteboard dishing out the formation and tactics for the day ahead; it was a small insight into what a footballer might experience before the match, running out of the tunnel onto the pitch to the roar of the crowd – well, not quite a roar but small cheers from our parents who travelled up. It was a day they will remember forever as that day they felt like professionals, with one of the players describing it as the best day of his life.

I always enjoyed the presentations and Christmas parties, as that was the time you really got to mingle with the parents. The talk would always revert back to football, but as the years went on, I got to know the parents a little better. At presentations, standing up and talking about the players was never hard as they all had such different personalities, some being serious, some cheeky and some just downright funny with their one-liners, but all caring lads when they were kids. The effort that went into those events was immense. It wasn't just our squad; we would arrange it for the whole age group, so anything between thirty to fifty kids. No one was left out, including the siblings; it was hard work for my wife and my football wife (who was a huge help over the years), both very special people.

At mini soccer we would put on a small tournament of our own which, like any other club that runs a tournament, needs a mass of helpers to make it happen, and again, like any other club, it always seemed to be the same faces. Our age group were superb; we used to camp over with some of the lads and their dads on the Friday and Saturday nights, and the boys would love it. BBQ fired up and freedom in a field with your mates kicking a ball around until it was dark; even then we would turn the cars onto the pitch with the lights on so they could play a little longer. The other managers in our age group and I would do the BBQ for two days straight without complaint and with plenty of laughs along the way. Our wives, some of the mums and some of the siblings would help run the refreshments stall, again without complaint and with some laughs along the way. It was all done in good spirit, and it all helped raise a good amount of money for the club, which was much needed as it helped with buying equipment and keeping the cost of the subs down. We always seemed to be lucky with the weather, which was a big help, and although it was exhausting at times it was all well worth every second of our time.

MJ

I did not manage children under eleven at any point so only had the so-called 'stroppy teenage years'. Don't get me wrong, they drive you round the bend sometimes, and as we know teenagers can be moody, hormonal, aggressive and way too loud! But I would not have changed it for the world; the kids I worked with for over five years were absolutely fantastic young people. The proudest part of those five years was, of course, how much they improved as football players and doing so well, but more seeing the fantastic young men they turned into at the age of sixteen and seventeen when I stepped down. Whatever small part I played in that journey makes me very proud.

I don't envy children in today's world. They often have more than their parents had in terms of material possessions and an 'easier' life in that respect, but they have it so much harder than their parents did in so many other ways. Personally, I do not like social media, I feel far more harm than good comes from it, but I know I am in the very small minority; rightly or wrongly, it's the most powerful force in today's world. It is everywhere and there is no escaping from it. For children in particular this is huge pressure, too much pressure at a young age.

We had it simple: three or four channels to watch on

TV and playing out on your bike or football at the park. Not always very exciting, but life was simple. Nowadays, life is twenty-four seven for a teenager; social media does not stop. Constant posts, photos and chat – it is relentless. Cyber-bullying goes on everywhere and children cannot escape it; little wonder more children are depressed and suffering with their mental health than ever before. We do live in a plastic and materialistic world, not helped at all by the media, who seem intent on children becoming adults at younger and younger ages. The stress young people have of keeping up with the latest fashions and looking the right way (especially girls) must be exhausting; there is no escape, not ever. I dread to think of the carnage if social media and camera mobile phones had been around when we were growing up!

Despite all of the above, in my (admittedly limited) experience, I found the kids to be an absolute credit to their families and themselves. Obviously, I can only talk of my own experiences, and I was very lucky. Even more impressive is that this was despite them being in an environment where many adults around were setting all the wrong examples. Of course, some kids are going to be rough around the edges and many think that they are real tough guys, but underneath they are all just children and when you get to know them and earn some trust, they are all good kids. The so-called 'bad kids' are always just a product of their environment; the vast majority of the time, standing behind a 'bad kid' will be a bad parent. I have always found that kids today are far nicer and more respectful than the kids when we were growing up!

Nowadays the boys I managed are men of nineteen and

twenty and I am still in contact with at least half the squad in one way or another. My son is good friends with several of the lads and I will have a couple of pints with them and a catch-up from time to time. Another couple became good family friends and will regularly come over for dinner with the family. Hopefully, I can still help them now and again with some advice or ideas in their career endeavours. I am also good friends with several of the parents more than three years on which is nice. This is the part of junior football that makes it all worth it: friendships, years later, because of football.

You are definitely more than just a football manager. With all the stresses of modern life mentioned above, sometimes children need someone to speak to or some guidance, especially if they don't have the most stable home life or don't have a parent around. I know lads that went through enormous personal tragedies, which was heart-breaking to see, but the strength of character and personality they showed was really very humbling.

My approach to training and matches seemed to be quite different to the style other teams in the club used to adopt and the way the club would encourage. I was never really convinced the older age groups could improve much technically, certainly between the ages of fifteen and sixteen. But in terms of tactics and game management, they really benefited, and they were becoming young adults, so it made no sense to use the same approach I used at under-twelves. Over years you would see junior teams playing in exactly the same way irrespective of the score and how long was left. It could be 1-0 with a few minutes left and the same team would have the whole midfield bombing forward as they would if it was 5-0.

I just tried to get the boys to think a bit more and having a plan B and C for different eventualities. Nothing complicated, just knowing when to commit more men forward or back and to react to the game. Corners used to be my pet hate. So few goals are scored in junior football because there is no plan at all. In our last season we started to be a bit more imaginative and have much more movement at the last second, and sure enough, we scored a few goals. It sounds a little cynical but I remember telling the lads to not sprint and retrieve the ball for a throw-on if they were winning; there was no rush! We would spend five or ten minutes at the start of each training session discussing the game before and the plan for the forthcoming game on Sunday, which really helped. Again, I was very lucky to have boys that did listen and gave it a chance; they improved so much.

When you look back, of course the big matches and cup finals always come to mind, but there are so many brilliant and often funny moments you have to smile at, especially when children copy the pros!

I have seen on several occasions goal-scorers point and look up to heaven despite having never lost anyone in their family or close to them! This is up there with lads scoring and running along the touchline cupping an ear in response to the non-existent fans giving him grief or putting their finger on top of their lips doing a 'be quiet' gesture. My personal favourite was when I watched a couple of lads about to take a free kick just outside the other team's area. One of them shielded his mouth with his hand whilst discussing who was taking it to make sure none of the hundred cameras could lip-read what he was saying!

Another time watching my younger son's team play, one of his teammates gave both sets of parents a really good laugh and exchange of banter. It was pouring with rain, the pitch was a mud bath, we were losing 9-0 with thirty seconds of injury time left and we scored a goal to make it 9-1. The lad who scored sprinted to the goal to get the ball and ran back to the centre circle with it, clearly thinking the comeback was on the cards – bless him, it was so funny. The final whistle went immediately after kick-off. The opposing parents had been respectful all game and we had been chatting throughout which was good despite the absolute thrashing we had received. It was good fun in the pouring rain telling them that 'they were rattled' and 'if the game had been another five minutes, they would have been in trouble'. It was always nice, irrespective of who won or lost, when parents could get along. It wasn't often.

In the early days for some reason our regular right back was playing further forward, and he found himself in the very unusual situation of having the ball on the attack not far from their corner flag. Having not played football for long and still getting used to it, his defensive instinct kicked in and, safety first, he kicked the ball off to give them a throw-in next to their corner flag!

In the same season, I had a really nice kid playing for our team who was good but had a tendency to not really listen or take in the instructions I would give him. On this occasion he was coming on as a sub in a really tight game and I spent several minutes explaining to him to stay on the right-hand side of midfield – even when the ball was on the left to keep his shape and not get drawn out too far. At least three times I said, "Stay on the right; don't go to the left." As the substitution was made, he ran on the pitch and sprinted to the left wing!

Anyone connected with junior football will know the classic 'it's 0-0, boys' after going a goal or two up to ensure concentration is maintained. One lad missed the meaning slightly, shouting out 'it's 0-0, boys' after scoring to make it 1-1!

In the later years, one of our lads was a very skilful player but developed somewhat of a temperament; I had to speak to him more than once about his temper, which was a shame because off the pitch he was very laidback. In his defence he had been fouled a couple of times, which the referee had completely ignored. It happened a third time, the same player. It was a bad foul directly in front of me and very close to the opposition manager. In full view and earshot of the referee and their manager, he told me, "Simon, I am going to kill him the next time he comes near me!" I had no real choice then but to take him off to cool down, with both the referee and manager looking at me to do something.

Sometimes the kids were not as smart as they thought they were, or maybe I was not quite as stupid as they thought I was! All I ever asked was that if anyone did something wrong, they were honest and admitted it. A couple of times there were issues along these lines where I knew who had stepped out of line because all the other parents and players had told me who it was. Especially with online group chats and social media, it is hard to get away with anything. As ever, it was only ever kids being kids, and once they owned up everything was fine; honesty was all-important. The old classic line which never got old, although I think I outlawed it by the last season, was, "I am not well/have a slight injury so can't come to training on Saturday but will be OK for the game on Sunday." I was actually happy for kids to miss training now and again; I never would decline anyone as long as they asked me. They were doing GCSEs, some were playing football for the school, we trained on Thursday, so it was not a problem to miss training now and again on a Saturday. But strictly no fake injuries or illnesses!

Neither my wife nor I were overly happy to get a call at midnight one Saturday from one of the lads whose lift had not turned up after a party and needed to get home! I'd had a few beers that evening so could not drive; my wife very kindly picked him up. She was very much part of the football family and so supportive throughout. Neither of us were going to let him walk home in the middle of the night.

Some of the best times were on tour in Holland. We went twice and, on both trips, I was so proud of the way they conducted themselves and represented the team. They were far better behaved than the dads – we spent most of the time in the bar! Although I was not too happy on our final night when, as well as half the team drinking all night, one of the lads had chatted up a Dutch girl in town during the day and invited her back to Center Parcs, where we were staying that evening. In the politest way possible I had to tell the poor girl she had to go back home, and I got lumbered with the cab fare!

In Holland, it was lovely to see them all getting on so well and really enjoying themselves away from social media and being online; it was proper old-school. They would spend hours in the swimming pool and slides and, of course, play football; it was really nice to see so many smiles on faces. There were, of course, the obligatory practical jokes; at one point I was called by one of the players asking if I could rescue him from the roof of his lodge as he'd been locked out by his teammates. I found out afterwards that on the second trip a few of the boys went on an 'unauthorised' trip into town to find some nightlife. I think I am glad I only found out a year or so later!

The actual football was a great experience as well, getting to play in proper grounds with stands and changing rooms. The facilities were amazing and a different world to what we had. After one of the games, the Dutch manager asked about a return game in the UK. It would have been great, but we could not really offer much in return. No changing rooms, no stands, not even a straight football pitch or goal nets without holes. It was also fantastic to see how the Dutch teams played in a couple of games; we chased a lot of shadows. Their coaching was so good and the way they played was so organised. They really looked after us as well; we made some friends and were made to feel very welcome.

I look back now and am so happy that the boys had so many positive experiences during their time playing football. It was not always easy continuing to stay positive and do things the right way when so much is wrong around you, but it was worth it. My son and his friends have some brilliant memories. I have a few too; it was an absolute pleasure to manage them all.

SC

THE DARK DAYS

My journey into football management was completely accidental, as is probably the case for many junior football managers. One day when my son was around ten, he asked me if he could go to a local football club to train and play. At this point he had never shown any interest in football and had never played but he wanted to try it as some of his mates played for a local club. In the town we lived in there were two local junior clubs; to avoid any complications or upset, we will call the two teams United and City.

I vaguely knew one of my son's friends' parent Mark (the co-author of this book) as I knew his son even at that age was well into his football and I knew Mark was a manager at United. I approached Mark during one school run and asked if I could bring my son down to training. Mark could not have been more welcoming and invited us down the following Saturday to training. I still have not forgiven him – that was when the insanity started!

It was very clear that even at the age of ten, boys who had been playing for a few years were ahead of my son and that particular year was very strong for football to the point that they already had three teams in our age group. He played a few games for the third team that season, which at the time was the last year of non-competitive football, coming on as a sub mainly; he even scored a couple of goals. The team seemed to have been put in the wrong level (the first of many such situations with the league) and they lost every match until the last game of the season when they drew a game, and we celebrated like they had won the World Cup, which was really good to see. During the summer more boys came down to train in our age group, some of who had played before, and we were further down the pecking order. Eventually it was decided to try and set up a fourth under-eleven team for the coming season which my son would be in.

The season started and it was evident that this team was completely out of its depth; my son was one of the more experienced players by then, by virtue of having kicked a ball a few times the previous season. Some of the lads had literally never kicked a ball; they were not ready to play competitive football against established teams, even in the bottom division. To make matters worse, they started off with only a squad of eight (it was nine-a-side football), which made it impossible to even compete. Regularly a player would not turn up and we would be playing with seven boys. It was thoroughly depressing, regularly getting beaten by rugby scores.

After a few games I started getting serious concerns around the structure around our age group within the club. We could not field a full team whilst the three higher teams had squads of thirteen or fourteen, meaning several subs every game. Although we were a new team (and admittedly not very good), we were not being given equal or fair treatment – at least give us a full team! The boys were eleven; being the poor relation was not doing any of them any good. Kids from the other teams were openly taking the piss out of our players and we would always have the worst area to train on with the worst equipment. It was all very unpleasant, and the club did nothing to improve the situation for us; they positively encouraged it.

They were managed by a guy whose son played in the top team and wanted to manage the fourth team to help the boys (which sounded jolly decent of him). He was helped by another parent, who admitted himself that he knew nothing about football, but in fairness to him he stepped up so that the lads could play, which was very good of him. This arrangement continued for about half the season until a couple of dramatic things happened which gave me the dubious honour of taking over as the manager of the fourth team of United and starting my managerial career.

One of the guys lost his temper after a kid from another team smashed a football into his face. I think it was the last straw; he was understandably completely fed up with the club's treatment of the team. Then it emerged that the other fella had not taken on this team (giving up seeing his boy play every week if games clashed) out of the goodness of his heart after all. For some reason, the fourth team had more mums than dads as parents, purely coincidentally; there seemed to be single-parent lads or just boys whose mum was able to be there more than the dad.

It was brought to my attention by a couple of the mums that the manager was using his position as the manager to contact the mums, go round to their house to 'discuss their son's football development' and proposition them to some one-on-one coaching (and I do not mean the kids and football). The words shit and doorstep sprung to mind, and he also had to go.

Not the first manager to be appointed following a scandal, I volunteered to take over. I had no idea what I was letting myself in for; I was badly out of my depth; I did not have a clue. One thing I knew I had to do was treat the boys much better than they had been treated so far. The first training session I took really did show me the mountain we had to climb. The other three teams were all given brand-new kits courtesy of sponsors. We had not even been made aware of ordering new kits and getting a sponsor. Yet again the poor relation: our boys had to watch the kits being given out whilst they wore third-hand kits. The dubious circumstances of the former manager leaving were also public knowledge, which reinforced the 'joke' of a team belief.

The first thing I did was sponsor the team myself (with money I did not have at the time) and made it very clear it was completely unacceptable to leave our team out from sponsorship opportunities and, even worse, to flaunt the new kits in front of them, when their self-esteem was already at rock bottom. That was the first of considerable amounts of money I gave to football clubs over the years. The kits cost around £300 (I could have bought it directly for that amount, but you had to buy via the club, and they charged £700 from memory). This was actually cheaper than what I would pay in future seasons, and to this day I know that none of the profit they made ever came back to my team. A rip-off and another kick in the teeth, but I was not going to have my team treated like the poor relation just because we were the weakest team on the pitch.

I then wanted to make us competitive to the point that we were losing by single figures and maybe could dream of getting a point before the season ended. The one problem I had was that I was clueless, absolutely useless. I hated drills and coaching exercises, and I hated dealing with parents, the admin and collecting subs. It was stupid to even try but I did not want to let the kids down; they had been through enough.

We did at least have a squad of ten by this stage, which gave us the luxury of a full team most games, and now and again we had a sub. One of the other dads helped me, fortunately, and we did OK; the 10-0 losses became 7-0 and then 4-0, and we were not far away from getting a draw or two. But the league does not lie and twenty losses out of twenty games in the bottom division tells its own story. Then, on a glorious day after the season had finished, we played a new team coming into the league in a friendly. I really fancied this one; I desperately wanted these boys to win a game.

We played really well; I think we sensed it was a fifty-fifty, and we had finally found a team we could match. No goals at half time and all my hopes of winning or drawing took a massive blow: the other team scored. My initial response was 'here we go again', fully expecting it to become a 4-0 loss. But we quickly equalised and then, with five minutes left, we took a corner; the keeper flapped at it and punched it in the air, and it hit our player on the head and went in. We had done it: we won a game at the twenty-first attempt. I did not care if it was a friendly, a new team we played – we WON a game. The boys were buzzing, parents were buzzing; it felt great – I was so pleased for them.

Despite the horrors of the season, I wanted to keep going. I was still clueless with training and drills, but I loved matches and was OK at tactics and setting the team up for matches. Most importantly, I got on well with the players. We were definitely improving and who knows? With a few more players we could win a match in the league and maybe even not come rock bottom.

We started preparing for the new under-twelve season early in the summer; there were more boys interested in joining and we had it agreed by the club (which I took with a very large pinch of salt) that we would get any new players coming in as we had the smallest squad by some distance. However, our best player from the season before and his dad, who was also my assistant, had left, which left two big vacancies, but we had some new faces, including a very good striker who had played at a much higher level before breaking his leg and being out for a season. He was mates with one of my players (whose dad also volunteered to assist me) and wanted a season to get back into football and fitness, which I was very happy to accommodate. We also got some other boys who had not played before but were really keen and looked pretty good at the level we were playing, so all things considered I was happy with my preseason transfer window!

Clearly sensing my optimism and grand plan of maybe winning a game in the bottom division of the league, the club once again put the boot in. A 'club official' took great offence at our new striker joining my team and told me, in no uncertain terms, that he should play for one of the higher teams, as he could 'get turned off football for good if he had to play at our lowly level' – nothing to do with the fact that he was also the assistant manager of one of these higher teams he would go to, of course. I explained that whilst I generally agreed that boys should play to the best of their ability, on this occasion he had been badly injured for a year and specifically wanted to play with his mate and ease his way back into football, which his mum wanted too. It was a one-off season and if it went well, I would be the first to help him push on to a higher level. It beggared belief that after being snubbed continuously and not even allowed a full squad the season before, they actually begrudged me a player and wanted to force a kid to play in a team he didn't want to play in without his mate who had invited him down.

In the end the lad's mum had to send an email to the club complaining about being pressurised by the 'club official'. Ironically, the same lad had a great season, got player of the year, scored loads of goals, and got his fitness and confidence back after the leg break. I helped him find a new team and encouraged him all the way at the end of the season. When we moved clubs the year after that he came back to play for us again and was brilliant for the next three seasons – a really great lad and a huge reason for the success we later had.

The 'club official' was not finished, though: he dealt with the player registrations, and after I gave photos of two of my players directly to his wife, to give to him to get them signed up for the start of the season, he claimed to have never received them. He also did not think to let me know that neither player could be registered for the first game of the season until I chased him a few days before the season started. When I had a moan and reminded him that we were on the same team, he told me that I should not have trusted his own wife to give him the photos, I should have given them to him directly, and that 'we are on the same team but it's a shame you don't know that'. The anger and spite, all because an eleven-year-old wanted to play with his mate in my team for a season after being in a wheelchair the season before after breaking a leg, rather than go to his team.

Not surprising with two players missing and a very hard first game, our hopes for a good start to the season were well and truly crushed when we lost 6-0. However, the boys did not give up and only lost the next game by a goal, and then the following week we won our first ever official game; they were brilliant. The celebrations and seeing the boys' faces was worth all the crap from the club. It was also satisfying as the team we played had a club house right behind one of the goals and several parents brought their beers onto the field right behind the goal and spent one half taking the piss out of me and the boys. Spectators were not even allowed to be behind the goal, but the referee did not fancy asking them to move – they were well on their way; it was a 2pm kick-off. I did make a complaint to the club to take up with the league but predictably I never heard anything again.

I think the glory of winning a game went to our collective heads: we lost the next game 8-1, which was great fun. However, we then went on a good run, won a few games and were holding our own going into the new year.

But the tensions with the club increased throughout the

season: we were still being treated like second-class citizens, still given the rubbish training areas, equipment and even kick-off times were always the worst time, with other teams always being given preference. The season before, when I took over, it was new to me; I didn't have the confidence to really challenge things the way I should have done. I believed all the 'it's about the kids' rhetoric and thought the best of everyone because, after all, they were 'volunteers' and giving up their own time so must be good blokes. But by then I could see it was not like that; there were way too many agendas and 'volunteers' making it about them.

At one point I was told (when I questioned why a new boy looking to join the club was not coming to us as agreed at the start of the season) that he had to go to a higher team as he would end up giving up football if he played for my team at our level. One division up, in the heady heights of division five (out of six), on the other hand, was perfect for him. This was a big club and many people within it were great – I knew quite a few personally, genuine people doing their best for the children. Even the other managers within my age group I got on well with, but there was something very toxic about the environment. It certainly was not a 'club'; it was a number of teams, each with a different manager, culture and way of doing things. I could not really blame the other managers for taking players ahead of us, they were doing the best by their team. It was the management within the club, the chairman and club officials who should have set the rules and made it clear to all the teams the process for the recruitment of new players, ensuring that all children were treated with respect irrespective of ability. Especially at such an impressionable and difficult age where children were becoming young men with all the emotions and pressures this change came with.

The second half of the season was dire: the excitement of winning a few games had long since evaporated, the boys were defeated and, in all honesty, so was I. To make matters worse my assistant stepped down; another parent stepped up for a bit, but it did not last – it felt very lonely. I felt so protective of the boys but was completely out of my depth. Losing game after game, the boys got very disheartened and stopped taking it seriously, and a lot of the team would spend most training sessions and even before games sodding about. I later realised this was very much a defence mechanism: if they did not 'try' or 'care', losing all the time did not matter.

I have to give huge thanks to Mark for the support he gave at this time. He was the one person at the club who had helped us from the outset and, despite running the first team, had given his time and support consistently. I was very stressed with it all and didn't really want to do it anymore but at the same time could not let the boys down, especially as there was no one else to take over. Mark came to a couple of games towards the end of the season to help me out and gave some good advice and guidance and we managed to win a couple before the end of the season, and with a draw in our last game we managed to finish just below mid-table.

It felt more like we had been through a war than a football season. It was a huge uphill struggle, but we came above several teams (albeit in the bottom division), we had been massively inconsistent, but if nothing else, the boys had proved that they could hold their own if they stuck to it. I was ready to call it a day, though; it had been stressful and unpleasant the majority of the time. I did not relish another season in the environment. I asked if anyone wanted to take over again and a new dad who had recently brought his son volunteered; we are still pals to this day. Although it became apparent quickly that I wouldn't be able to step away completely, it was too much for anyone completely new to everything, so we did it jointly. The one positive, which did mean a lot, was that the boys wanted to stay, so my efforts could not have been completely for nothing.

As the season approached, I had my first taste of other teams 'folding', which went on to feature so predominantly in the area in our age group. One of the teams in our age group at the other club in the town, City, folded, whose manager later became my assistant. This meant that suddenly there were a dozen more players looking for a team, which should have been good for our team as we were meant to get any new players as we hardly had the numbers to field a team. Naturally, this promise was immediately broken, and the other teams all had their pick of players and even the manager of the team that had folded became an assistant manager to one of the other teams. Once again, we were left high and dry.

However, after recruiting the players they all wanted, we were 'given' a couple of players from the higher teams as they had to make way for the new guys. Finally, we were useful to the club (and they call the professional game ruthless). I remind you again the boys were twelve at this point. The boys that did join were great and settled in well despite the shoddy way they had been treated. We did lose our star striker, who left for a premiership team with my blessing. Obviously from a selfish perspective I did not want him to go, but I told him he should for his own development. Clearly, I was in the minority in putting the players' development and welfare ahead of my own team. But we got three or four new players in and at least had a full squad.

We started off quite well, but almost identically to the season before by the new year we were losing more than we were winning and it didn't work with the joint managers. By this stage, the tensions with the club were reaching breaking point. More of the same: 'don't forget you are the fourth team, know your place', etc, yawn, yawn.

The breaking point came with new 4G training the club had signed up for at a school in a nearby town. It was a twenty-minute drive for parents. Not ideal, but early on a Saturday morning parents were OK with it. However, different teams were allocated different times for an hour from 8.30am through to 11.30am. Naturally, we were given the crap 11.30am slot that no sod wanted, and it was suddenly 1pm by the time the boys had trained and gone back home, taking up a fair part of the day. Understandably parents were not very happy; some could not even commit to it, as they were used to training at 9.30am five minutes away. To add insult to injury, we only got a third of a half of a pitch to train on and we were given the middle third! For a team in the bottom division the ball tends to go out of your training area or pitch a fair bit. I would spend an hour getting our footballs from the teams on either side; it was a joke. Yet again no consideration for my players, my parents and my team.

We stopped going training at this new venue every week and went to the local park sometimes where there were pitches. I told the chairman that we were not after any money back; we just wanted to train properly at a reasonable time. The chairman then removed our training slot completely – even though it had been paid for.

It was time to call it a day: my approach to child welfare and equality were the polar opposite and completely incompatible with the club's. I was disgusted at how my players and parents had been treated. One of the dads suggested moving to City as, following one of their team's folding (and most of the players joining teams at United), they only had one team in our age group so we would immediately go from being a fourth team to a second team. More importantly, it had to be better than where we were; it had been awful. I was now well and truly invested in this junior football lark. I figured that despite all the problems and the abysmal approach to child welfare from the club, we must have been doing something right because boys still wanted to play for the team. I also now knew exactly how not to do things. From now on it was going to be different; I wanted the boys to have all the support and good times they had missed out on. We were going to build a proper team; I had a new lease of life and, probably for all the wrong reasons, was hooked.

City could not have been more accommodating: immediately we could see that they placed much more emphasis on child welfare, and they also encouraged the under-fourteens (which was the age group we were going on to) to go on a tour at the end of the season, usually to Holland. They were very keen on the kids having good experiences and it was not all about winning, which was music to our ears after the toxic culture we were escaping from. In a further twist of fate, the other team in our age group had fallen out with the club, over some football kits of all things, and had left to join a different club. We were going to be the only under-fourteen team going into the next season. No more fourth team, which we were sick to death of. Without kicking a ball, we were the first team and no longer anyone's poor relations; psychologically it was a massive boost and a very exciting time.

After agreeing to join City and telling United we would be leaving at the end of the season, which they accepted with good grace at face value, in a final parting shot from United the club 'officials' did not invite my team to the end-of-season presentation. I contacted the chairman when I realised all the other teams had been given a time slot and was told that we had been left out because we had left the club to join our fierce rivals. I could come and pick up the lads' medals, but we were not welcome to come to the presentation. I explained that the parents had paid their subs and that included medals and end-of-season player of the year trophies and were still all players and parents of United. Once again, child welfare was ignored: his club, his rules, we were not welcome. I went out to the local trophy shop and bought squad- and player-of-the-year trophies for the team; I did not want the boys to lose out. Yet more money the club had off us.

It was horrible; in fairness, they were consistent to the end. Yet again middle-aged men who should know so much better using their position of authority to take their personal grievances out on children. I also learnt for the first time about this ridiculous rivalry between the two clubs – 'fierce rivals'?! This was children playing football; there should not be any rivalry; it really should not matter. Why not accept it was good for all concerned for the boys to move to a different environment and simply wish us well?

It was hard to comprehend the club's conduct during that period; it was the sheer hypocrisy of it all, not putting the kids first ever whilst repeatedly claiming to be champions of child welfare and pillars of the community. We could do things much better; for once it could be about the kids and football, not adults who had their day thirty years ago – me included. More importantly, make it a team on and off the pitch, for parents and players to be part of something, to go on tour, have social events, for the boys to experience good and new things. Football in itself was only part of what it could be. If I was going to do this thankless task, which is mostly a ball-ache, let's do it properly.

We spent the summer holding trials and trying to build a full squad (finally); it helped massively being the only team in our age group at the club. The whole environment was nicer, and we were able to do it our own way. The good news kept coming when the third team from United folded and we were able to recruit a few of their players – no big surprise given the way things were ran at United. Going into the season, we actually had a full squad and were looking like a proper football team. Not to mention United had gone from four teams to two teams, which I have to admit I found very amusing, especially when I thought about all the overpriced subs the chairman was not now going to get.

It was a grim time all round; now the boys are grown up we can look back and laugh at how rubbish it all was, but it certainly was not funny at the time. The one positive was that it showed me the blueprint on how not to manage football teams and how not to treat the children. I would be OK as long as I pretty much did the opposite of everything I had seen. It was a shame because other age groups seemed to be ran better and there were some good managers and coaches within the club, but our age group at that time was poisonous. This was further evidenced by the fact that within another year, Mark's first team playing in the premiership moved to another club and the last remaining 'second team' folded the year after.

There were all sorts of shenanigans going on off the pitch, constant rumours about money being syphoned off. At one point one of the top officials set up a company and was charging the club to do work at the club, even though there were volunteers who would do it for free. Sponsorship of kits was charged at double the actual price. Trophies could not be purchased through local businesses; it was all about 'preferred' suppliers – all very shady. It seemed a long way from a grassroots community football club. I don't know how much was true, but at best it seems incredibly misguided and naïve for anyone to ever put themselves in such dodgy-looking positions. Either way, we were cutting our losses and were out of there.

SC

THE BAD

Most junior managers will tell you that the most rewarding part of managing a junior football team by a country mile is working with the kids, helping them to improve at football and, most of all, helping them develop as people and helping them with life generally. They will also tell you that the worst part of managing a junior football team is dealing with the adults, most commonly the parents. These are some of the experiences one or the other of us encountered with some observations and reflection now we are 'retired'.

I am sure all parents at one time or another would have been given some work that their child had done at school. A painting, a story, a card, something they had made for you – you know the sort of thing. We all know that often that painting is terrible; you probably don't even know what it is meant to be if they don't tell you. But because it is something from your child and you love and support them, you tell them how great it is.

Now imagine receiving that painting and immediately shouting at your son, telling him he has done it all wrong. Telling him the drawing is not good enough and making it clear you are not happy with this 'performance'. Pretty disgusting, but change the painting to a football game and it happens every week. I have seen children as young as eight being berated and screamed at by parents and even coaches on occasion. Games have been abandoned due to punch-ups at under-eight games. By the time kids are under-twelves and -thirteens, the gloves are off: it's fair game to shout and scream at players as a matter of course. Complete insanity; it would not happen in any other walk of life and be accepted as normal.

I was very lucky: all the kids I ever managed were great and most of the parents were good people and generally appreciative of what my assistant and I were doing for the boys. In my last season the vast majority were fantastic, and I am good friends with several parents and players to this day. Some of the behaviour from other teams' parents over the years or other games I watched was at times horrendous. I would be literally speechless that an opposition manager would allow this to happen.

With my own set of parents, it was more the lack of support and cooperation when you are trying to help the boys and improve the team on and off the pitch which could be a kick in the teeth. I always believed passionately that the only way to really improve on the pitch was through team spirit and togetherness, both within the kids and importantly also their parents. A sense of family is very powerful, especially when some youngsters don't have a stable family unit or have suffered horrible family tragedies. Security, and being part of something, is massive, and this can only really happen when you have parents engaged in the same culture and backing you up.

In my last season at under-sixteen level, I really did get lucky. Where we had so many boys wanting to join us, we had more than enough for two teams and another parent bravely volunteered to set up a second team. A few boys moved between teams and some new faces joined both teams. For my team it was just one of those lovely times when everything clicked; the new lads were a brilliant influence on the existing players. Likewise, the parents were generally fantastic, proper football people who I immediately could see would be a positive influence on everything we were trying to do, and they really did buy in to what I wanted. Their kids had generally had a tough time the season before, yet more local teams in our age group had folded and they wanted a change, to enjoy football again and be part of a proper team. The mix was wonderful, the players were great and the vast majority of the parents were not only supportive but wanted to contribute and be part of it. Suddenly if we did a social event, they would all turn up; when we booked the tour to Holland, three quarters of the team had parents wanting to go as well. They helped out with lifts and sponsoring kits; they put the kids first – it was refreshing. The boys achieved great things in that last season, they were an absolute credit to themselves on and off the pitch, but the parents did their bit too – well, most of them!

If you do get to a position where parents are supportive of the manager and reinforce the key messages and behaviours to the children as well as help other parents and kids out when needed, usually as simple as lifts to training and games, you are halfway there. In the early days I would have to beg a parent to take one player as I would be picking four up and had no space – whilst getting to the ground forty-five minutes early to put up goals on my own. If you then get to a situation where players and parents are actually starting to like each other, and you can make social arrangements and spend time together other than on a Sunday morning and work together to give the kids outings and experiences (and importantly there are no bad apples constantly moaning and causing problems or even just refusing to engage in anything), you really are in a lucky and uncommon position. The positive energy and behaviours are contagious; they rub off between parents and players alike, and then when you start improving and winning matches as a result, it brings further positivity as well as renewed confidence which in any level of football is massive and improves players further. Boys then want to come to every training session as they are happy and enjoying being in the team.

I was advised numerous times to have a big squad of sixteen or seventeen as boys will not always turn up and at that age are unreliable, but they could not have been more wrong. We had too many players; they always turned up. Sometimes I wished they were a little unreliable as getting everyone a game was the biggest challenge of all when you have five subs.

It sounds simple, but it is incredibly difficult to get the support of fifteen sets of parents or certainly the twelve or thirteen needed to drown the negative ones out. Some parents will never be happy; they will spend season after season complaining about game time, the manager, the results, the fact that their boy is being placed out of position or other boys are not good enough. The list is endless; nothing will ever be good enough.

In my first two seasons, I failed miserably to inspire any such unity. The boys were great; we had improved to the point that we won a few games (and lost a lot more), but most of the boys had never played – they had done brilliantly. But the parents were just not interested in getting involved at all. The sheer suggestion of socialising and mixing with other parents seemed to terrify some parents. I would suggest a drink in a beer garden after a game so the kids and parents could mix, and they would look at me as if I were from another planet. Some parents are just not interested: they would just drop their kid off, wait in the car for an hour and a half, and take him home. It is not really in the spirit of a community club/team, but it takes all sorts. Where I did take offence was when the same parents who contributed nothing at all to the team would still feel entitled to complain if anything did not meet their approval.

There were some difficult times over the years, and you do sometimes see parents treating their children in ways you really don't agree with, and you do sometimes find yourself being disrespected and your time and kindness being abused. It is normally not meant in a deeply offensive way, more just inconsiderate, but you need to have a thick skin and not take things personally, which is often very difficult.

With your own parents, the most annoying occurrence is trying to organise something. A match, a training session, a team outing, even a tour away on holiday. It should be so easy: set up a WhatsApp group and send a message with details asking for responses. Everyone gets the same message – two-minute job. Sadly, around half the parents will ignore you completely, so you send a chaser message a few days later. A couple will respond, so you are down to four or five responses outstanding. A third chaser goes out, which might get another response. Finally, you send a stroppy message often referring to the fact that you are busy and don't really have time to ask for the same thing five times, especially when this is being done for the benefit of their child. That usually does the trick, but sometimes you still have to chase the odd one up. Before you know it, you have spent four hours over the course of a week texting and chasing parents to simply get their agreement for you to do them a favour and look after their kids in some capacity! That was where I struggled to not take things personally.

When I was a kid playing junior football, our long-suffering manager would have had to call fourteen sets of parents just to give an arrangement for the next match. We now do the same in a single group message on WhatsApp. It has helped in many ways, with key messages and information; it is a fantastic means of communication which all managers will gratefully use to the maximum. But the downside is people cannot communicate personally anymore and it has become acceptable to completely ignore messages and calls, even when it is beneficial to their own child. In some ways it was easier back then because there were no mobiles and no call screening so everyone had to answer the phone; it was not possible to ignore someone (unless you unplugged the phone completely and then no one could get through to you). Those fourteen calls perhaps were quicker as there was no option to ignore anything and claim to be too busy to send a five-second text.

I remember wanting to leave a junior team when I was

a teenager. My parents made me phone the manager and personally explain my decision, man to man, so to speak. Nowadays kids would just not turn up again and even a text is too much to ask and the parents do not bat an eyelid. They genuinely think it acceptable to completely ignore a person who was more than good enough to take their son under their care for months and sometimes years.

As with much of society, the existence of mobile technology, the internet and social media, particularly when it comes to texts and messaging, has caused far more harm than good when it comes to common decency and respect. Parents would think nothing of sending a stroppy text complaining about something you have done wrong (in their eyes), telling you how you don't know what you are doing and generally being quite unpleasant, but would not dream of saying it to your face. Similarly, they will completely ignore a text needing a response. This is not limited to football; it is everywhere. People are very brave with a mobile phone in their hand and their Facebook or Twitter account open.

An early memory was a time after a training session. I had spoken to one of the boys during the session because he had been messing around at matches and at training. It was no big deal: nice lad, quiet word, 'don't do it again' – all done. I had just got home when a text came up from his mum unhappy that I had spoken to him and 'told him off'. I read it within five seconds and immediately called, knowing she would still have the phone in her hand. I was not going to have a text debate when it could be resolved in two minutes. But she would not answer. I called again a couple of times; still she would not answer. That was very much a sign of things to come: parents over the years would sometimes have plenty to say by text but simply could not say anything of the kind in person. Having an actual conversation is somehow seen as 'confrontational'.

End-of-season presentations were always very interesting as you would often see just how ungrateful some parents were. To this day it blows my mind that as a parent you can let another parent look after your kid for hundreds of hours all year, without a penny being charged, and you still cannot bring yourself to buy a bottle or box of chocolates to say thank you at the end of the season. Please, for any parents reading this, even if you think your manager is useless, you clearly still trust him enough to supervise your most precious thing in the world all year round, so he cannot be that bad – buy him a box of beers now and again. Trust me, it is a thankless task most of the time; the appreciation of players and parents and small gestures go a very long way.

At under-fourteen level we had just had a brilliant year: we were a new team and won our division; the boys were buzzing. One of the mums tried to organise a collection for me and my assistant; she told me afterwards that several parents could not bring themselves to give anything at all, once again ignoring the texts. It should not matter if you win something or not, some appreciation for the time and commitment is only right, but when you do have a perfect season it still happens! What sort of example is that setting for the boys? It is not a good look – a little gratitude, please!

Arranging trips and tours away can bring the worst out in parents. There is something quite disrespectful, when you are arranging something very nice for the kids, to still get ignored and messed around by the parents. Most were OK, but I have had parents repeatedly ignoring requests for money to pay for the trip or even just passport details needed for the flights. I even had parents committing to trips and then pulling out without paying their deposit, meaning I had to stump up the difference (or increase the price to everyone after giving a final quote). The best example of a completely ungrateful parent was when we were working out dates for the weekend of the tour and we had to consult with the school to make sure all exams were finished on the weekend we wanted to book. Our kids all went to the same school, and we got clarification back, which we all agreed was adequate. However, not content with the assurance provided, one parent requested on the group chat that I personally provide an undertaking guaranteeing the exams would be finished. I had to try and explain that I was not actually a travel agent. Or even a full-time football manager. I was doing my best to give her son and all the others a great experience.

The awards are good fun as well; parents get so political it is crazy. I had to stop doing the 'parents' player of the year' and instead go with 'players' player' (but I would not give the players any notice; I would keep them all separate at training with no warning so they could not discuss and get all the names at once). I saw parents vote for boys that clearly were not the player of the year as they thought their boy was in contention and they did not want to risk voting for another contender. Despite my repeatedly telling parents they could not vote for their own son, they would still try! More worryingly, you would get parents not voting for clearly the best player because they did not like his parents personally or the boy was not friendly to their own son. All sorts of skulduggery would go on.

Parents are so fickle; when we were moving clubs and setting up a new team, various boys were trying out and we played a couple of friendlies and one lad had agreed to join us. We played one Sunday and won 2-1; it was really good game, and things were looking to come together. I received a text after the game from a parent: "Thanks for taking _____ on, he is really enjoying it, it's lovely to see him playing with a smile on his face again."

A week later we played another friendly and lost 2-1 and another text the next day from same parent: "Sorry, mate, but _____ won't be joining, he just does not think the level and other players are good enough."

I explained that these were friendlies, and we did not even know who was in the squad yet and some boys had been away, but that was it. There was no discussion; in seven days and one friendly game we had gone from brilliant to terrible. Ironically, a few weeks later the lad was desperate to join again. The grass is not always greener. Another lad at the same time simply stopped coming to training completely and his parents ignored my texts; this was after I had picked him up several times to take him to training and matches to help them out. It was only when I texted and said I would be round to their house the following Saturday to pick up the team shirt he still had that I received a reply. Another time, one of the dads approached me and, without a trace of irony, told me his wife wanted to help me with subs but he wasn't letting her, as he didn't want her wasting time on stuff.

A common theme I saw in several teams was a distinct negativity towards the most talented players. Invariably the best players can have a tendency to be selfish sometimes, perhaps not passing when they should or trying to do it all. This continues into adult football and many strikers at any level are not always keen to share the glory! But often in junior football if there is a particularly talented player it can sometimes be that they don't trust another player is going to keep the ball or score the goal if they do pass, and from a child's perspective the chance of scoring is greater if they try to take on another couple of defenders and go alone (as well as the glory, no doubt). Of course, we want our teams to pass, and it is a team game, but it is more than understandable for a child to see it that way.

I always believed that a player with that special talent who can do things no one else can is a positive thing, and great skills and goals should be celebrated, but many parents and managers really try to stifle it and highlight all the things other than the very special things the player does offer the team.

One dad at a game I was watching continually shouted his son's name out to get his attention, in order to give some brilliant tactical advice such as 'get stuck in more'. You could see the lad was sick and tired of it, and he started ignoring his dad as he clearly just wanted to get on with his game. Undeterred, at one point the dad shouted his name a dozen times, increasingly louder each time, until finally he relented and looked over. All of this just for the dad to give a thumbs-up and say, "Well played." Another example of the obsessive need some parents have to interfere; they just cannot let their child get on with it.

Just the mention of parents and money in the same sentence breaks me out into a cold sweat. Most parents are fine: they pay their subs and anything needed as requested, no problem at all. A few over the years took the piss; you find yourself chasing the same parents every single time, whether it be subs, training fees or payment for trips away or socials. Invariably you just get fed up with chasing. I was always so busy and often you pay it yourself to avoid the tiresome process every time. If a parent or player is genuinely struggling, I was always happy to help, but when it's parents who you know are not struggling it really does irritate you. It's not fair, but again, you cannot take it out on the kid who has done nothing wrong, so often you end up covering it yourself so he can be included.

When I talk to fellow managers and ex-managers, I know I got off very lightly with my parents. Witnessing parents from other teams on match days was a different world completely. Not a single player at the levels we were managing has gone on to play professional football. A couple, with the right breaks, could play semi-professional. The level of ability and commitment needed to make it as a professional is ridiculous; we all knew our children would not end up playing for West Ham and England. And I am sure parents must know this, especially as the most vocal ones purport to be football experts. So why on earth would you scream and swear like a madman, abusing your child and other children, when they were trying to play a game of football?

We always wanted to win and took it seriously, there were probably times we took it too seriously, but the personal abuse, digging out a player for a mistake they made, is too much. Watching a group of men screaming out to the world that 'he doesn't want it' whilst referring to twelve-year-old boys about to make a tackle. Or shouting to his own boy to 'take him out' or 'hurt him' in reference to stopping one of our players on the ball. I have never understood it and never will.

Mental health, especially in recent years, has become much more recognised, especially in men. Tyson Fury should take much credit for bringing much-needed awareness to men, and it is now much more acceptable for men to suffer and talk about mental health problems. If the heavyweight champion has been there, there is no stigma for anyone to need help. When I look at the anger many men have whilst watching professional games and then even junior games, I do worry that many men are suffering mentally. Let's face it, you cannot be feeling great if you think it acceptable to scream abuse for a couple of hours at kids every Sunday.

During Covid and lockdowns there has been an increase in stress with considerable pent-up anger and that is reflected in the professional game. In the last couple of seasons, there were many problems with fans at games; at times it seemed more like going back in time. There seems to be more disenchanted and angry men than ever. It might be anger that they didn't make it as a football player or, perhaps more likely, just angry because life has not worked out the way they wanted it to. Watching the football on a Saturday and screaming some abuse is a release, the one opportunity all week to release the anger and frustration. When this behaviour is also happening at junior football games, it really is a problem, and surely the mental health of our children is also crucial. They need to feel secure and see the right behaviours from the adults around them; they are all products of their environments.

I have seen a full-scale pitch invasion where at least twenty parents invaded the pitch to get to the referee, calling him a cheating cunt, the usual nice language in front of children. I saw another parent in an under-thirteen game threaten a manager and 'offer him out' in the car park after game (and waited for him after the game). An under-fifteen game between two local teams (within the same club) was abandoned due to parents fighting on the pitch.

Linesmen are routinely abused and threatened when they do step up to run the line. Some parents go the other way and will do the line in order to cheat, and any forward pass is flagged up – anything to win. I have seen a referee abused and berated throughout an entire game by the other team's manager, two assistants and all his parents. When they did not win the game, it continued after the final whistle and the referee sent off the manager. You then had his wife and other mums screaming to him that he was a cunt and 'are you going to fucking send me off now?', all in full view of both sets of under-thirteen players.

Ultimately clubs obviously don't want this conduct and will have safeguarding policies documented, but they are not physically able to deal with these incidents. Who is going to remove a team of rabid men screaming obscenities and threatening violence? A fifteen-year-old referee is already terrified. A league official who is never at the games. It cannot be policed, and clubs will always shy away from dealing with incidents. How are they going to tell a manager, tell a parent, he is banned? It takes months for the clubs and leagues to deal with even the most straightforward of cases, and no one wants the grief, so it just carries on.

Too many parents want to carry out their failed football careers through their children. It is the dark side of the crazy football bug we all have. They honestly believe that they 'could have made it' and were brilliant in their prime – before they discovered 'beer and birds' and 'did their cruciate'. None of this was true; they usually played at a similar level and were as far away from the premiership as our sons are now. But in their mind, they know it all and honestly believe they know better than the kid's manager and coaches when they are screaming out their cliched and meaningless instructions.

I have even seen parents tell their children to 'ignore' what their manager has told them as he 'does not know what he is talking about'. How confusing is that going to be for a child? It has been shown time after time: children want their parents to support them and be there at matches. But they do not want them shouting things out and getting involved. I have seen kids cringe and in tears after watching their dad's behaviour, and managers I know personally picking up the pieces, dealing with sometimes already very troubled children.

Parents will all have different views on how things should be run. Whether they have any right to have an input whilst contributing nothing to the team is arguable. Many parents will start off being more than polite and say something along the lines of, "As long as my child is happy playing football then so am I."

This is actually a complete lie in most cases; it often translates to, "I am happy as long as you pick my child every week to start, he plays in a position he wants to play in, the team is winning most of its games and we as coaches value him as one of, if not the most valuable player in the team – if not then we won't be happy." The tightrope you have to walk sometimes is bizarre.

- If you don't win games – 'my boy is too good for this level'.
- If you do well and win games – 'my boy is not getting enough game time' or 'you are playing my boy out of position'.

This does not mean every parent is a pain in the arse; they certainly are not. You need different types of parents at football. Although I am sure it would be a much easier environment if no parents came at all. But this is not the case and most probably will never be the case.

Some of the type of parents we have encountered are below:

1. I Could Have Been a Pro Parent

Another lie in football. If you could have been a pro, then why are you not a pro? Living every player's fantasy, playing in front of huge crowds in stadiums around the country, earning loads of money – oh yeah, that's right, you couldn't have been a pro. Maybe you played at a good club level, maybe even got to semi-pro level, maybe even won a few trophies along the way. Well done you. But come on, a pro? These parents like to think they could normally run the team better than the coaches, don't offer much help but have plenty to say when the team isn't winning matches.

2. The Helper

This parent is happy to help out, will arrive early to help put the goals/nets up, will run the line if needed and does this more than any other parent during the course of the season, has an opinion on some things, but you don't mind listening as they are so helpful. These parents are very much needed and like gold dust, as without their help it would mean even more work for the coaches.

3. The Silent Type

Gets their child to every training session and match on time, replies to all messages promptly, doesn't engage much with the other parents and often stands away from them on their own. Doesn't help out, doesn't criticise, doesn't get emotional and stand there shouting at the team, stays nice and calm during the match, cheers and claps in the right places. This is almost the perfect parent just behind the Helper.

4. The Screamer

This parent is very emotional, does not mean to come across as aggressive, and he would call it passion. Will offer instructions to players on the pitch, will call for most decisions from the ref, will stand their ground if other parents from the opposing team are a little out of order, will have to be told by the ref to calm down and also the ref will ask us as coaches to have a word with them to calm down. This parent probably doesn't mean any harm but can create the wrong environment with the way they come across.

5.   The Sponsorship Parent

This parent thinks they are Roman Abramovich because the company that employs them have kindly offered or been asked to sponsor the kit or equipment in some way. Now in grassroots football every team needs sponsorship; it's vital to help get kit and sometimes training equipment to ensure the team can actually just get out there and play. But this is mostly done out of pure generosity and not a reason to claim they now own a piece of the team. We were lucky to have some great sponsors who were very generous, but you always get one, don't you!

6.   The Wind-Up

This parent does not say much; they get on with most people until they get sussed out. They are pretty quiet but will say things like 'I wouldn't have that' if someone's child gets subbed or moves position. Or 'that wouldn't have happened if your son/daughter were on the pitch' after a mistake from another player who is on the pitch. These parents are not helpful at all, just loading the gun for other parents to fire.

I am sure people will say there are many other different types of parents, but I'm guessing most teams will have one of these in their squad. I mean, it takes all sorts in this world.

Is there such a thing as a perfect parent? No would be the answer, although some can be very pleasant to get to know and I have made a few – and I mean a few – good friends through the parents. Should parents be allowed at football matches? It is a difficult one: many parents are no problem, and why should they be punished because of the actions of others?

Personally, and perhaps somewhat radically, I would not allow parents to watch the games. It sounds harsh, but if (as it seems) it is impossible to control parents, it is the only option. In other sports, you drop your son or daughter off and let them get on with it with the coach/teacher, for instance tennis, gymnastics, ballet, golf, swimming, etc. Imagine telling a gymnastics coach that they don't know what they are doing or shouting abuse at some of the kids taking part. Obviously, the key difference with the sports mentioned is that they are not team sports. But in other team sports such as rugby or hockey, you don't get anything like the same aggression and anti-social behaviour we see every week at football.

It is easy to say that it is a 'class' thing, that rugby and hockey players are more educated or more likely to be from a middle-class background rather than working class, which is more associated with football. But this only partially true: many children playing rugby have exactly the same type of parents with similar backgrounds as you find at football. They have it in them to behave just as badly, but it is not the way things are done. On the pitch players respect and talk politely to the referee; they generally do not argue with decisions and even after kicking each other senseless shake hands and leave everything on the pitch. Similarly, parents do not attempt to shout at and abuse players or officials; it is just a completely different culture.

However, perhaps there is some hope. A friend's son is a very talented goalkeeper and was selected for a local professional team's academy. At this level, the parents are made very clear that no form of shouting, coaching, criticism or abuse of players, other parents or officials is acceptable. They are welcome to watch and enjoy the game, but it stops there – no interference. And it works; it could not be more different to the typical Sunday-league experience. This is not because the parents of more talented kids are naturally much nicer and respectful; it probably has more to do with the fact that their son will be asked to leave the academy if his parents don't fall into line. If a club see that a parent will be a problem, they will be ruthless and let the lad go; after all (from a business perspective), thousands of kids would do anything to get the same opportunity.

Perhaps the same parents dream of their son making it to the top and funding their retirement with the millions that can be earnt. Perhaps they just don't want to spoil their son's football experience and the opportunity they have. Whatever the reason, if there is something at stake, something to think twice about before being a loudmouthed moron, it works. So clearly it is possible to happen at all junior games, but a carrot or stick is needed. And until they are found, I would keep the parents away and let the children enjoy their football.

SC and MJ

Some first-hand accounts of dealing with parents follow, which will probably strike a chord with other junior managers reading this.

FIRST EXPERIENCE WITH A PARENT

Most people when they get involved at grassroots football have no real idea what they are letting themselves into when running or helping to run a team – I certainly didn't. Luckily for me the guy who had already put himself forward to manage the team had also previously managed his older boy's team for a number of years so was almost a seasoned pro with how to deal with things. He was also on the committee at the club which was a bonus for our team. I was a little hesitant with my full commitment at first as I'm self-employed and worked a lot of Saturdays when the team would be training so made it clear I wouldn't be there every week for training, but this didn't seem to bother the manager much as I just think he was grateful someone had come forward to offer some help.

I had zero experience in coaching, especially coaching kids, so it was back to the drawing board for me to learn how to approach it; for the first month or so I was ball and cone collector. I had some input but not too much at first as I did not want to step on anyone's toes. As the season got underway, I started to give some input as he gained more confidence in the fact I was sticking around. It was the under-six age group and we had started playing seven-a-side every other week which was good for the kids as it eased them into football as well as the parents and trained every Wednesday and Saturday.

I am the type of parent who likes to get involved, not scared to put myself forward but also willing to let others take charge and help out if needed. A chance came up to get some free tickets to go and watch a Southend United league match (they are our closest professional team). I thought the kids would love it so took the opportunity to start arranging the day out.

I must have had about three to four weeks to arrange the trip – plenty of time, so how hard could it be? First job was to get all the parents' numbers and store them in my phone for a group text; I kept the parents updated with relevant info. I went to Southend United's ground to pick up the tickets after I had liaised with the club, who were fantastic; they even gave us more tickets than we needed so we could invite some of the players' siblings along as well. I must have sent around five to six different texts to the parents asking if they wanted their child to attend, how many kids were coming, about train times, etc. Some parents were great with replying, some were a little slow and some never replied but spoke to me in person or their child did.

So after one training session just before we were due to go to the Southend United match, I was walking up towards the car park where the parents were standing when a parent decided to start to dig me out in front of the rest of the parents. I am not sure if they felt they could belittle me as I was quite a bit younger than they were, but they accused me of not including their son in the trip. I cannot remember exactly what the parent said, but there is a time and a place to sort something out, and in front of everyone is not the time or the place. In my opinion a quiet word face to face is the kind of thing most people would do, not a raised sarcastic voice digging me out in front of everyone.

It turns out I had made a mistake when putting the parent's number in my phone – I had got one digit wrong, so they were not getting any of my texts, but when I showed them my phone it was clear their name was included in the texts, although the wrong number was in my phone. I held my hands up, but it obviously was not intentional and the child in question had been telling me all along he was coming to it.

Well, that was the start of the end of the relationship with that parent; they complained about the position their child was playing in, even though the child seemed happy and contributed greatly to the team and scored goals, and they would generally moan and be negative about everything. I actually liked the child; he was polite and always listened when we were talking, just a good kid. But the parent had decided to have an issue with me, no matter what I did. It was personal and very pathetic considering the time I was spending on their child.

One Sunday the parent hit an all-time low when we were playing an away match. My lad started the game playing at the back as we were one defender short, so he filled in – not his normal position but as he was one of the most adaptable players it seemed to make sense. It was the wrong decision: we did not start the game well, going behind quite early on and struggling to get up the field and create any chances, so we swapped another player to play at the back and moved my son back to his right-wing position.

This changed the game: we started to create some good chances from the right and managed to pin them back; my son was having the game of his life so far, was causing havoc every time he got the ball; he scored and set two up and we won the game comfortably. The players were coming off and patting him on the back saying how brilliantly he had played. Even as we walked towards the parents some said to me it was a man-of-the-match performance; anyone who knew a thing about football could clearly see he was head and shoulders above that day.

At the end of every match, we used to do man of the match;

this was decided by the parents whose child had received it the game before. Sod's law, it was the parents who had taken a personal vendetta against me. It was their opportunity to do the right thing and show that it wasn't personal. Sadly, they did not want to take this opportunity; after a silly little speech about how well everyone had played they gave it to another child. You could see all the other parents' faces looking shocked and also embarrassed. I am not taking anything away from the child who did get man of the match that day, but he wasn't the best player on the day; he even said that my son deserved it that day. It was all quite unbelievable that a another parent could do something like that. To take a small amount of glory from a six-year-old child to get one over on me. It was so pathetic, I actually felt sorry for them.

After that season they decided to move their child to a so-called better team than ours, but when the leagues were put out the child's new team was put in the division below ours; we even played them in a cup match and easily beat them around 8-0 or so. As I walked back to the car after the match, passing the child's parents, all I said was, "Unlucky," with a big smile on my face. I guess karma can be a bitch.

A Junior Football Manager

THE WORST JOB IN JUNIOR FOOTBALL

I walk over to the touchline where the dads are standing usually around ten minutes before kick-off. As I walk over some edge away, suddenly remembering they left something in the car. Others suddenly receive a call and take their mobile phone from pocket and put to ear. I am left with two or three guys still willing to acknowledge I exist. I say, "Can someone run the line?" One of the dads suddenly remembers an ankle or knee injury (he cannot remember which it is) which prevents him from occasionally jogging up and down half the football pitch. Another is too hungover (which may at least be true). If I am lucky one dad (often the same dad as a week before and a week before that) will reluctantly agree to do the worst job in junior football.

Over the years, the hassle of sorting out a linesman for the game on the Sunday was a bigger challenge than the actual game. Managers all over the country will tell you that the question 'who's running the line today?' will raise your blood pressure instantly. There is no doubt that it is not the easiest sell. After all, you are signing up to ninety minutes or so of grief and likely abuse without being paid a penny. But the game cannot go ahead without a linesman.

I never understood why it had to be so difficult and it was something parents repeatedly let me down on. It is hard enough training the team twice a week, dealing with the club, the league, lifts to training for kids whose parents cannot or will not take them as well as actually taking the training and arranging the match on Sunday. Surely parents could take this one job off your hands and give you one extra thing to not worry about?

No chance.

It is not difficult, if you have, say, twelve dads in a squad (probably more). If each parent does two games throughout the season all matches would be covered, and each dad has only had to ruin his own enjoyment of watching his son play once every four months or so. The phrase 'if everybody does a little, no one has to do a lot' could not be more apt.

Sadly, most dads point blank refuse, and if you are lucky, you might get two or three guys doing it. There will be a hundred reasons why a dad cannot do it; some of them include:

- I've done my ankle/knee/cruciate – often the same one that prevented them making it as a pro.
- Feeling rough today – getting over cold/cough/flu/hangover.
- I do not know the rules – despite watching football games for the last forty years.
- I do not know anything about football – probably true but as above.
- I do not feel confident doing it – but they are confident to shout and scream all sorts throughout the game whilst watching it normally.

Other dads literally just run away or simply stay in the car until the match kicks off; it is quite pathetic watching it play out.

Some managers even end up running the line themself, which really is outrageous and hugely disrespectful to the poor sod; has he not got enough to do? That was my line in the sand: I was never going to do that. It got so bad I would just put the flag down where the parents were and say, "We cannot go ahead with the game without it – I will leave you to decide who is doing it amongst yourselves."

In the later years I found the best solution was to throw money at the situation and we would pay a young lad (older brother of a player) to do it. The parents then had the choice:

pay £10 per month for the linesman or don't pay and run the line for two or three games. I think my parents had a few quid; the vast majority would happily pay rather than do the dreaded job. Although some parents were not happy because at one point our young linesman was getting more than the official referees, which they thought was too much. I partly agreed, but what can you do? It was simply supply and demand.

Parents of other teams who did the line were appalling. I had to speak to a referee once because the linesman literally did not understand what offside even was; he just put the flag up whenever asked. I had to beg the referee to get the other team to at least have a parent who knew what offside was. It really is not a nice job; we had our linesman threatened by the other team's parents and abused for an entire game on a fairly regular basis. Sadly, we are back down the same road where it is completely normal to expect abuse, which of course explains the lack of take-up. But at the same time, if everyone does a little at least you only get abused twice a season.

I became a complete hypocrite after I 'retired' from management. I also became part of the problem in the last game I did when I offered to run the line for my younger son's match. They were playing the other team in their age group within the same club. Bragging rights at stake; apparently some of the parents did not get along either. Just my luck – why could not I get a nice easy match against a gentle team? If such a team exists.

In the first half their 'linesman' flagged wrongly three times when our striker had a one-on-one. Two were not even close; he was that rapid, he made up five yards in two seconds. It was horrible and their noisy parents were loving it and then, to make matters worse, the other team scored with their first shot of the game. It was 1-1 at half time and the second half was largely without incident until their striker was played through; he was level but certainly much closer than the three calls against us in the first half. I know I should not have done it; I know it was against everything I stand for in junior football, but we should have been 4-1 up if they had not cheated. So, my flag went up.

Not liking the boot on the other foot, their parents went crazy. I thought their coach was going to attack me. The other team had cheated three times; I was not going to let them win the game and be rewarded for this. Probably not my call to make, though. I decided after that game to become one of the 'stay in car until kick-off' parents, once again perpetuating the problem. In fairness, I think the thousands of hours over the years I had put into junior football gave me a legitimate pass and the right to watch my other son play without a ton of abuse. But then again, all parents have their reasons to avoid doing the worst job in football.

A Junior Football Manager

UNHAPPY DAD

The lads were having a warmup when the coach and myself were both looking around thinking, *Where is our striker? We are kicking off in roughly ten minutes.*

We were playing at a summer tournament and were the first match on. The texts had already been sent out during the week to arrange times to meet, giving us plenty of time beforehand for the very reason that we were in the first match to be played. As the team finished warming up, we went through the starting line-up with the lads. As we were doing this, we could just about make out our missing player in the distance strolling across the field; as he got closer you could see he had no socks, shin pads or boots on, just his sliders while carrying a bacon roll and drink in hand. OK, so he was late – that is no problem, it happens, we all wake up late, get stuck in traffic or whatever, no big deal.

The team went out on the pitch and the game got underway; we had two or three subs that day so could rotate the lads to get some good game time and hopefully progress quite far in the tournament. Obviously, our late striker started as a sub so he could finish his bacon roll and drink then could get the rest of his kit on. As he sat down on our subs bench his parent must have spotted him and started to walk around; we did not notice any of this until we heard, "Have you got a season ticket for that bench or what?" We turned around and it was the striker's parent. If I am honest, I thought it was quite a good line coming from him. It continued: "Come on, get your stuff, we are going; I haven't come over here to watch you sitting on a bench all day." Wow, we were two minutes or so into an all-day football tournament and the parent had already thrown his toys out of his pram.

I turned and asked him politely to leave and to return round to the other side of the pitch. One of his favourite words was 'victimisation' – apparently that was what this situation was. We didn't have any other parent of the lads who started as a sub coming round accusing us of victimisation, and the other lads had been there around thirty minutes or so before kick-off fully kitted up without a bacon roll and drink in hand.

He told his lad a couple more times to get his things while I told the parent to politely go away and stop embarrassing his son. After a stand-off the dad eventually turned away and started to walk away. I turned and looked at the lad, who was slightly embarrassed, and said, "Listen, it's up to you, mate, if you want to go with your dad then that's fine, but if you want to stay that's also fine – nothing will affect you in this team, so it's up to you."

His reply to me was simple: "I just want to play football." And stay he did.

Unhappy parent walked round to the other side of the pitch and was clearly slagging me off to another parent who was new to the team as he probably knew the rest of my parents would have told him to shut up. The lad had no problem being sub and probably didn't have any breakfast so clearly wanted to finish his bacon roll.

After a couple more minutes the parent left without his son; it was no problem as one of us would drop him home as he quite often relied on lifts to training. The sad thing about it all was, the team played brilliantly that day, reaching the final but just losing out in a closely fought match; the lad also had a really good tournament, scoring some good goals, and his dad missed everything. All because of his own arrogance. I think the lad learnt a bit of a lesson that day about timekeeping and to arrive on time in future, kitted up, minus the bacon roll and drink in hand.

On another occasion in one of his son's early matches for us soon after joining we were playing a team we had beaten the week before 3-0 and we were confident that, although they were no mugs, if we played well, we would win. It started out more competitive than the first match and early in the game he made a late tackle trying to block the defender from clearing the ball and caught the defender on the follow-through. This happened right in front of us so just to the side of the other team's coaches. As it happened, their coaches started shouting at the ref for a red card. The ref that day was a young lad, probably around sixteen to seventeen years of age, and straight away pulled out his red card and he was off. My coach and I were shocked, at worst a yellow card, but it wasn't even that in our eyes; we had seen a lot worse over the years go unpunished, so to be shown a red at that age group was a shock.

You cannot blame the ref, as to have two fully grown men waving their arms around screaming for a red card must be intimidating, so I assume he panicked a bit. If I were to criticise, or I would see it as being constructive criticism, he should have taken a breath and the outcome may have been a yellow at worst – who knows? As our player walked off, I remember our coach turning to their management and saying, "Well done, you two got him sent off." They did not say a word.

We were down to ten men trying to console the poor lad, who was saying he had let the team down. That was not the case; we always made it clear that we won together and lost together, and anything in between we could deal with. The lad's parent started walking over. No problem; it is understandable that a parent would want to make sure their son was OK if they had just been sent off and was clearly upset. But he was not coming over to console his son – he said straight away, "What's he been sent off for? This is victimisation. Give me the ref's name and number – he will be hearing from my solicitor in the morning." Our coach told the dad to be quiet and stop embarrassing himself. So the poor ref, who had just been screamed at by a couple of forty-year-old men, was now being threatened with a call from a solicitor in the morning, being accused of victimisation. No wonder there is a shortage of referees in grassroots football.

Our main concern was for the lad, letting him know that he hadn't let the team down and at half time his teammates also reiterated what we had been saying. We ended up losing the match 3-0, a bad result for us, but in my opinion, it showed what a great group of lads we had, all sticking together that day, and we went on to have a brilliant season which parents still talk about to this day all these years later.

His dad ended up walking away and the referee never did get a call from his solicitor the following morning. Maybe he had realised what an idiot he had sounded, but then again, I know the man and I am pretty sure he would have been pleased with his performance that day.

A Junior Football Manager

NEW BEGINNINGS

Moving to City really was a huge breath of fresh air. We actually felt part of the club and we were the only team at under-fourteen level, so there was no pressure anymore. After a false start with one assistant, one of the other parents whose son had joined the season before agreed to help me – I will call him Bob. I could write a book about Bob: one of these fantastic characters you get in football.

The first day I met him, he turned up with his son, smoking a roll-up and on crutches; within half an hour, the crutches were discarded, and he was helping with training – I don't think he even asked me if he could help. After initially telling him he had to leave me to it, I realised just how enthusiastic and how much he really cared for the team. Could talk the hind legs of a donkey with his football stories and drove me mad much of the time having to listen to them, but what a top bloke, a real rough diamond. He would help line the pitch, put goals up, give lifts – nothing was too much trouble. Although it was the blind leading the blind most of the time.

We used to train at a nearby park on Saturday

mornings. I think one of our strikers was having a bad day and somehow missed the goal so badly with a shot it went sideways off the pitch for miles into the river. A while later it happened again: another player had smashed it off the pitch into the river. The players had a look: no sign of the balls; we accepted the loss. Bob had other ideas; he suddenly disappeared, and he went for so long, I forgot he had gone, and we finished the training session which had around half hour to go. We were just giving instructions for the game the next day when Bob emerged from the river. He was covered in mud and God knows what else; he had scratches on his face and was soaking wet, looked like he had been through hell and back. But he had two footballs with him, declaring, "I don't give up on a ball." With commitment like that, I was sold; he was my assistant. We are good mates to this day.

From day one everyone really seemed to want to do well and be part of a proper team. It was a such a random mix of players: some had hardly ever played; a few had some experience, having just had two seasons in a row of folding with City and then United and were now back at City – the politics was exhausting but I was not complaining. I just wanted to be left alone and try to make up for all the lost time and negativity at United. Maybe my son and his mates could start enjoying their football without adults ruining it. The 'new dawn' continued with the best signing of all when my star striker from two seasons previously wanted to join us again, which was brilliant. He had played at the higher level for a season but had not enjoyed it so wanted to come back and enjoy his football again.

The boys generally got on well and it was a really nice team spirit. Obviously, there are always a few disputes and disagreements between players, especially at that age with all the egos and hormones flying around, but it was a wonderful group of lads and generally a great environment.

For training we simply started looking at fitness much more rather than making it all football-based. We were not going to make a fourteen- or fifteen-year-old much better technically, in the way you would if they were six and seven. I had also noticed that many players were not that fit and would be knackered in the last quarter of a game. So, we tried to get the boys fitter; the best way of doing this was when a local boxing club kindly allowed the team to train with them. Now those guys really are fit and as hard as nails but so respectful and it was such a positive environment. The team gained so much from that training (despite a lot of moaning at the time!). It made a huge difference; we scored so many goals in the last fifteen minutes of games. We actually invited one of the boxing coaches to hand out some of the awards at the end of the season; it was a brilliant boxing club.

We would also take ten minutes out at training to actually plan a match and at least have an idea of what each person's job was. All simple stuff; it just was not something being done at the time or the 'approved way'. In all honesty the general technical ability of most teams at our level was not great, so a little fitness and organisation went a long way. We tried to use common sense: when we played the best teams with the quickest strikers, we would move my 'star striker' back, who was as quick and skilful as anyone. Massive credit to him for doing this and putting the team first; it was exactly the message we were trying to put across. We did not have the best players, but we did have the best team.

After the epic battle mentioned earlier with our big rivals, we won Division 6 of the local football league at under-fourteen level in our first season. We did not care what division it was: we had won something. I could not have been happier; the lads had done so well. It was lovely seeing them gain confidence as the year went on and become friends away from football in many cases.

We had very little involvement with the club; they were very much focused on the younger teams, which suited us perfectly – it was great to be left to get on with it. The club meetings with the 'club officers' and other managers were largely irrelevant, but we tried to do our bit and attended a few.

The only slight concern came at the very end of the season at the presentation, which was for all age groups. We had invited one of the boxing coaches along with my friend Ricky, who was a professional footballer playing in the National League, to give out the trophies. About five minutes before we were due on, the club chairman, who I had never really spoken to, approached us and asked if he could hand out the championship trophy we had won. I politely explained that we already had a couple of guests to do this and thought nothing more of it. A few days later, over a beer with my mate who was one of the club officers, it turned out the chairman was offended I had declined the offer and had been having a moan to him about it. It seemed very petty as there was absolutely no offence meant; we had already made plans, not to mention no one knew who he was – we had not had any contact with him all season. At the time I was completely unaware that something so innocuous would be held against me later down the line, but I am sure it was – egos in junior football can be incredibly fragile!

The perfect season was rounded off by the tour to Amsterdam we had planned all season. We got a coach all the way from Essex, over the Channel, through France and Belgium into Holland. I don't know how our long-suffering coach driver did it judging by the noise and smell of that coach.

On the football side we played two Dutch teams. Both games were in proper stadiums similar to maybe a national league side; it was amazing. The first team was outstanding; they absolutely ran rings round us – we lost 4-0. The way they passed and moved was so polished. Afterwards, talking to their coaches, they told us that all the age groups played the same way; there was a very clear football ethos, and all teams would play the same formations and styles. It was very impressive; the coaching was a step up from anything we had in junior football, and it made complete sense to train players from a young age the same way, with all managers promoting a consistent way of playing. In junior football in the UK all we had ever seen was individual teams within a club, all with completely different coaching and styles. It was not surprising they were so far ahead of us, not to mention the wonderful facilities they had; from what they said there is much more investment in proper sporting facilities.

The second team we played were weaker and had a few boys in the year below; they were a much newer team, and you could see they were more at our standard. We won that match and scored a few goals to the delight of everyone involved. Not everyone can say they scored in a Dutch football stadium.

Off the pitch was an absolute blast from start to finish; we stayed at a Center Parcs, so the boys had plenty to do when not playing matches. The parents got nicely acquainted with the pub onsite; it was the perfect place to take them. We even found a local bar that was happy to accommodate sixteen fifteen-year-olds whist watching the FA Cup Final. It was so chilled; we made a vow to go back. My assistant Bob was on fine form throughout the trip. At one point we were all in a downstairs bar playing pool with very steep stairs. To this day I do not know how he managed to fall down the entire flight of stairs whilst not spilling either beer he was holding; it still gets talked about to this day. On the way there after too much early-morning junk food at the ferry port, the coach had to make an urgent stop and the boys got a ringside view of Bob running off to be sick!

We were not given long to enjoy our newfound success; we had so much support, especially in the league decider, but within weeks the players were being told they had only won in the 'bottom division' and the 'standard is shit'. As ever United was making mischief, Mark's premiership team moved to another club, but the remaining team was approaching our players with the promise of playing three divisions up (the third division of six). Another team was also apparently being formed, which was going to also be better than us and wanted our players. It was so tiresome; the lads would not have even cared what division they were in. They'd had the best season of their lives, won the league, been on tour, made many new friends and now adults were interfering and making it about them. None of them were ever going to make it as professionals, so why not let them play and carry on enjoying it? It was relentless, and despite everything going so well, a couple of the boys were considering leaving.

I was forced to take drastic action to settle this ridiculous situation once and for all. Firstly, I asked the club to apply for us to go up three divisions to the third division. We had come on so well and even played a couple of teams at that level in friendlies and held our own. I was convinced there was not much difference between the teams outside of the top couple of divisions, despite the very noisy claims to the contrary that it was a 'different level completely' by the teams trying to poach our players. It would have been better to have taken it more slowly, but there was no choice: the lads were fifteen by now and they did not want to hear another year of being told they were playing at a shit standard. Miraculously for once the league actually granted our request.

We then arranged a friendly match against the last remining team at United which was already playing in the third division. Now we were in the same division, I knew that if we beat them, it would stop the 'taping up' approaches for good and we would be left alone. There would be no argument left about 'levels' and all that other crap. The boys really fancied it; they were unstoppable and smashed them 6-0. In less than a year away from United, the difference was incredible.

Job done: revenge was very sweet and finally some much-welcomed peace and quiet for a couple of weeks without any football before we came back for the new season. It felt like we were running a military operation as opposed to a children's football team sometimes; it was ridiculous that the kids playing football seemed such a small part of it all. The surrounding bullshit was becoming tedious. But despite the adults, the boys had a wonderful year, and we were on the up.

SC

THE UGLY

In this chapter, we have given some true accounts of real-life situations witnessed first-hand by junior managers and referees which have brought out the very worst behaviour in junior football. These are beyond some aggressive parents shouting the usual abuse or a weak referee helping his preferred team with a dodgy decision. They are beyond a manager favouring his own son over other players or even a league turning a blind eye to another child welfare incident as it's one of their mates.

This is where it went really wrong and the adults involved in the various areas of junior football let our kids down very badly and demonstrated behaviours which set the very worst examples to our children either through aggression and intimidation or a complete lack of integrity and honesty. We are under no illusions that far worse than even this goes on; this probably seems tame compared to some situations in other areas and leagues. The scary thing is the volume of such incidents; they are happening up and down the country every week, hundreds of times. Every junior manager and referee will have similar experiences, some far worse; these incidents are far from isolated. This should not be happening anywhere, let alone in front of children in the name of junior football.

THUG DAD

"Hi, mate." It was one of our coaches calling me from his car after the match we'd just played. I was in the car park after the match talking to the referee.

"You OK?" I asked.

"Mate, can you do me a favour and come back to mine? That prick is following me home."

This had started months earlier. An opposing parent who just seemed to be a very angry man all the time. Moaning, shouting and contesting every decision all game – you know the ones. It was our first match against them and we were at home, always a good even match between us played in a good manner, apart from this fella. It was not long into the game, and he was off; we could hear him clearly from the opposite side of the pitch, screaming and moaning about every decision that went against their team. There were no other parents or coaches from the other team moaning and shouting, so it was safe to say the referee was not getting things wrong.

The referee was only a young lad so maybe he thought he could intimidate him into getting decisions for his son's team. To be fair to the lad he didn't seem at all fazed and was having a good fair game in my opinion. When the parent started shouting and getting even more angry, I looked over to their manager, but he did not seem to be bothered. Why would a manager not react to one of his parents behaving this way?

1. He is so used to it that he doesn't see or hear it as being unacceptable behaviour at a kids' football match?

2. He does not want to cause a scene at a kids' football match and wants to concentrate on managing his team?

3. The parent is a nutter who will only kick off if confronted and throw his toys out his pram if he does not get his own way?

I knew their manager quite well as we had always played each other in friendlies in preseason and often met at tournaments over the summer months; he was a lovely bloke to be fair. I had a lot of respect for him and his team as they had always been a top side and he managed to keep a good regular core of players, which isn't always easy to do.

So, Thug Dad was mouthing off and maybe it wasn't my job to do or say anything, but I can't ignore something that is completely out of order. I looked over to the parent and shouted, 'Hey,' then held my hand in the air and closed my hand as if to say close your mouth. What a big mistake that was: this was obviously the parent who throws his toys out his pram easily. He straight away started to walk around the pitch with purpose, looking very angry, almost going red in the face as he was starting to boil from the inside.

My son was sitting on the subs bench with two of our other lads; as the angry man was walking round, my son said worryingly, "Dad, he's coming round."

I looked at the opposition manager and asked him, "What's going to happen here?"

He replied with something along the lines of, "For fuck's sake, not again – what's he playing at?"

The guy started to get closer and started shouting at me, "Come on then." He must have thought he was in a scene out of the football factory rather than an under-thirteen Sunday-league football match. He said it again, this time adding the word 'cunt' at the end – remember, this was in front of twelve-year-old lads and where we played our home matches was in front of the club's café where parents and children from other teams could see and hear what was going on. I chose to ignore him as my coach and their manager told him to go away. He shouted again, "Come on then, me and you in the car park." Oh my good god, I could not believe I was hearing something so immature and embarrassing coming out of a middle-aged man's mouth. What did he want me to do, go and have a kiss and a cuddle behind the bike shed? I turned and looked at him and just shook my head in disbelief and continued to watch the match. I thought this guy was not right in the head; what is going through someone's mind to make them walk seventy to eighty yards around a kids' football pitch swearing, to ask the opposing manager for a fight in the car park in front of parents and kids? It was disgraceful.

He eventually left after a few minutes and headed off to the car park on his own, maybe getting ready for the fight that was never going to happen. After the game I half expected him to still be in the car park waiting for that fight, but he wasn't, thankfully. Maybe he saw sense at how stupidly embarrassing he had been, I don't know. But now we were playing them again at their ground a few months later.

It was a nice sunny day and, as mentioned earlier, we usually had good close games when we played each other, but on this day, we were superb, getting the better of the match. One of their players was getting very frustrated; by this point we were 2-0 up. This lad was on the wrong end of a throw-in decision from the referee and picked up the ball; as our player went over to the line, he held out his hand to gesture for the ball. At that moment the lad threw the ball straight into the face of our player; our player didn't react, luckily, and the referee blew his whistle and came straight over to give the lad a talking-to. The lad was showing no interest and the ref brandished a yellow card. As the lad walked backwards away from the referee he started to clap and say, "Well done, ref, well done." Straight away the whistle went again, and the lad was shown a second yellow card followed by a red and ordered off the pitch.

We had had this ref a good number of times and this was the first time I had seen him brandish a yellow card, let alone a red card. So you can guess who his dad was – you got it, Mr 'come and fight me in the car park'. Inevitably he started going mental on the side-lines before walking onto the pitch ranting and raving in front of all the parents and kids, swearing his head off. Their manager and coach were telling him to calm down; our coach was telling him to calm down, which he didn't seem to take too well. This went on for some time before he eventually headed to the car park with his son and another family member and decided to leave. Thank Christ for that; at least we could get back to the football now. We went on to win the game convincingly, as you would expect when a team is down to ten men, but fair play to our opponents: they never gave in and fought to the final whistle.

After the final whistle hands were shook and mutual respect was shown. After the match, the parents slowly started slipping away, including our coach and the other team's parents, while my wife, my son and I were left talking to the referee. I thanked him for refereeing the game and said how well he had handled a very difficult situation. This was when I received my call from our coach asking me to meet back at his house as this guy was now following him. This dad had left the kids' football match, driven home, dropped his family off then returned and waited for our coach to leave and follow him and his family home. Wow, it suddenly took on a whole new very creepy and menacing level. He'd had at least an hour to cool down and he still thought it a good idea to follow through with his actions. Most people would cool down after a few minutes, maybe even ten minutes, before realising something like this is not a good idea. But not this guy: he went full steam ahead.

After I took the call we jumped in the car and proceeded to head back to the coach's house; there were a few different routes you could take and I ended up getting to his house a couple of minutes before he arrived, followed by another one of our parents who had spotted what was going on and decided to follow as well. Our following parent said the guy had pulled into the shops around the corner from our coach's house; we had a little laugh and joke about it but said if he did return to call the police and explain what was happening. This guy had driven miles out of his way, around a twenty-minute car ride; surely you would have come to your senses by now?

Making sure the coach was happy, we left his house and headed off home; our following parent left first and pulled out of the turning. I couldn't get out straight away because of oncoming traffic so there was a gap between our cars; as I pulled out I could see our parent down the road when suddenly this guy pulled out behind him and started to follow him now. My wife rang his wife who was also in the car to let them know and to say not to drive home and go to the shops near their house, where there would be plenty of people to hopefully deter him from doing whatever he had planned.

We ended up behind Thug Dad, but he had not spotted us as he had never seen our car. We pulled up to some lights – our parent was at the front, Thug Dad was behind him followed by me. The boot popped open and out got the dad. I was thinking, *For Christ's sake, what's going on?* He walked to the back of his car, where he had a set of golf clubs in the boot; he reached in as if to grab one the clubs. I was thinking, *I am going to have to get out of my car and try to stop this*, when just then the lights started to turn green. He closed his boot, jumped back in his car and set off in pursuit. Blimey, that was lucky.

The dad still hadn't noticed me directly behind him, which was a good thing; our parent pulled in to the local shops as planned, the dad drove past and I followed in to the shops' car park and had a chat with our parent, saying, "Let's stay here a few minutes so he is well out the way then you can carry on home." We both parked facing the road; the shops were on an estate which went around in a big circle roughly three miles round in total so wouldn't take a long time to drive round in a loop back past the shop, and that's exactly what the dad did, not only once but three bloody times in total before finally giving up; it was insane.

Our parent ended up calling the police to report what had happened so something was on record as this guy was clearly not quite right mentally and capable of anything. A full-grown man doing this because of something that had happened at his son's under-twelve football match.

Why would a man act like this? Maybe work stress, home stress or financial stress – all of these could play a part in a person acting out of character. Unfortunately for this parent it seemed it was just his character, as once I had spoken to a few managers/coaches who knew him I found out it was unfortunately a common occurrence, and the parent was still allowed at kids' football matches. Why hadn't this been reported previously? How had he not been banned, and what sort of example was that setting for his son? If things do not go your way in a football game, resort to violence.

The police made a record of our parent's concerns as we were due to play this team again in a cup match; the police said it would be noted. When I got home, I had to call their manager to tell him what had happened – to say the least he was gutted and embarrassed but not overly surprised it was this particular parent. He said he had had enough of this managing lark and wanted to give it up; it is hard enough running a team let alone dealing with this sort of shit. Thankfully, he did not give it up because of one idiotic parent.

When their manager spoke to the parent about what had happened, he almost brushed it all off, saying he was only messing around. MESSING AROUND! So you leave a match after your child gets sent off then decide to come back and wait for the game to finish then begin to follow the opposing team's coach home, then one of the opposing team's parents home, driving around for maybe two hours or so and a good few miles away from the town you live in, and you try to laugh it off.

A few weeks later we played this team again in a mini cup competition. We both got to the final, and when we turned up, I spoke to their manager, who seemed still slightly embarrassed about his parent's actions and said neither he nor his son would be playing or attending the game that day. Well, that was a relief; to be honest it had been playing on my mind all week. I went over and told our parent who had been followed that they were not attending the game, and everyone seemed a bit more relaxed once they heard this.

Thankfully, the game was played in a good spirit, and we were beaten by them. They seemed like a different team, more together; maybe this was because this parent was not at the match screaming at every decision or at every motion of play; maybe this dad caused the team to feel nervous in case they messed something up and ended up on the wrong end of some abuse from him. It cannot be nice hearing a fully grown adult shouting aggressively all match when you are a twelve-year-old just wanting to play football.

This goes back to how a parent's behaviour can impact not only his own child but the rest of the players on the pitch and the game as a whole; this one person had managed to get me thinking about what to do if he had turned up and he had started again rather than concentrating on the kids. I know I had spoken to my coach about the possibility of things going wrong rather than the football. Their manager must have been relieved to hear he was not going to come to the match, but could he have been completely certain he wouldn't just turn up? I am not so sure, and what would he have done anyway if he'd kicked off again?

A Junior Football Manager

FOOTBALL IS FULL OF SNAKES (EVEN JUNIOR FOOTBALL)

One of the worst mistakes I made whilst managing in junior football was to ask my team's former manager to become my assistant. The warning signs were there right from the start. I was just too stupid at the time to see it.

I was contacted by a player who wanted to join us who had been playing for the age group above as an underage player. He did not like the team or manager and claimed they were about to fold. It emerged the boy's dad was the original manager of my team which had folded two seasons previously. They had gone to another local team the season before, which also then folded at the end of the season and was now back at our club in the older age group, which was also apparently about to fold. I struggled to keep up at the time, but the bottom line was that whatever team he managed or coached seemed to fold, which was not the best track record.

A couple of the parents whose lads had played under him previously also warned me that he was slippery, and it did concern me how quickly they were willing to go over the current manager's head by approaching me. The lad himself should not have even been making contact with me directly under child welfare/safeguarding regulations. In not one of my cleverest moments, despite all the hefty baggage, I agreed for them both to join and the dad to help with coaching. The lad was a good player, the dad seemed harmless enough and he loved doing coaching drills, which neither my assistant nor I enjoyed doing or were any good at. What could possibly go wrong?

By the next season having three of us involved in managing and coaching the team really was not working. Definitely too many cooks. Since returning to the club, he was fixated on becoming a club 'officer' and getting back in with the club after folding the team a couple of years previously. The club was clearly grateful for another volunteer, so they had long since forgiven him for this. He was so worried about pleasing the club and his own son that the identity of the team changed considerably the following season. It was my own fault: when things happen gradually you do not notice as much and then suddenly the team was unrecognisable from the season before. He was also pushing for his son to become captain, which I wrongly agreed to, allowing him to share the role with the existing captain at the time.

By the following season, sadly my assistant had gone so he became my assistant. I still thought he was a good coach, but I had vowed to myself to go back to my own way of doing things, more like it had been, and I was not going to get talked into any decisions about players or anything else. This did not go down well at all.

He wanted his son to be captain, and when I made clear I

had someone else in mind, I pissed him off big time as well as his son (who I suspect he had told would get the captaincy). His wife was even more pissed off; she never spoke to me or my wife again.

The gloves were now off; he did everything he could to get rid of me and to take over. He would simultaneously be supportive of me in front of my players and parents whilst reporting back to the club how terrible I was. Towards the end of the season, I confided in a few of the parents and would actually send incorrect info out on the group chat to confuse him or confirm my suspicions, as we knew every last word said within the team was going back to the club. I even told him I was stepping down over a silly issue near the end of the season to see his response, which confirmed all my suspicions: he could hardly hide his glee.

Everything I tried to do for the team, he would push back on. The worst example was when we tried repeatedly to book the end-of-season tour to Holland. Selecting dates became an absolute nightmare: picking a date after GCSEs and after end-of-school proms but before the summer holidays started and families started going away. It only left a couple of weekends, but on both weekends a player had a mum with a big birthday. Typically, his wife was one of them; they were not going away, but she refused to back down. The other lad who could not make the other weekend had plans to go away for his mum's birthday.

It went on for hours and days; it became an absolute pain. With all options exhausted, the thing left was to spin a coin and one lad unfortunately would have to miss out. The other lad accepted this within a second; he didn't want his mates to lose out just because he could not go. However, my assistant and his lad were very vocal in making it very clear that if he could not go, no one should go. I had explained ample times that not all lads got to go away each year; for some it was the opportunity of a lifetime, but I might as well have been talking to a brick wall; they just did not get it. At the eleventh hour the other family changed their entire plans for the mum's birthday trip for the sake of the boys. The whole team chipped in to buy some flowers to thank her for her selflessness; it really did sum up everything good about the team and everything wrong about the coach.

The backstabbing continued. I should have asked him to step down; he just could not be trusted. He had his big chance one Saturday towards the end of the season. We had a perfectly good training session, and the team was buzzing for a big cup quarter-final the next day, our biggest game of the season so far. All sorts of dishonesty and sneakiness went on that day. We said goodbye after having a final chat about the game the next day, but by the time I got home, several parents had contacted me. It had turned out he had finally made his move to replace me, with the blessing of the club, who had emailed all my parents saying they had asked me to leave. I had shaken his hand barely twenty minutes before at training!

The parents made it very clear to the club that they were very happy with me as manager, and that with the season ending in a few weeks, their actions were completely unacceptable. Luckily, I always kept all email communications with the league and club, so it was impossible for him or the club to give a genuine reason for me not to be the manager. Not to mention the fact that he had backed every decision I made so he would also have to be sacked if there were any genuine concerns. The timing was so cynical and divisive; the boys were so excited about the cup run they were on, and it was so depressing that he would rather us lose the biggest game we had ever played by creating absolute carnage within the team less than twenty-four hours before the big match.

But he was never going to succeed; parents and players alike were all so united. It was seriously emotional witnessing how loyal and how strong the team had become. Justice was served when the parents and players resoundingly supported me and then karma arrived with some appalling weather the next morning, meaning the game was postponed and we lived to fight another day, when we were much better prepared. The coup had failed miserably, and he hid away for a week, not replying to emails or calls from me or anyone; it was pathetic. And we won the rearranged quarter-final.

Even after the season the mischief continued with the end-of-season awards, and I already knew from before that he would do anything to ensure his son won something. Everyone had been brilliant, but it was fairly obvious who the winners deserved to be; there were a few guys who for different reasons had been amazing. As well as the player of the year, sportsman of the year and most improved player of the year, which were provided by the club, I had also added parents' player of the year and players' player of the year, manager's player of the year and coach's player of the year. I wanted as many guys to win an award as possible.

Our captain won both the players' and parents' awards, which were voted on so had no input from us. The player of the year was agreed no problem and my manager's player of the year to me was an easy decision: our converted striker who had been brilliant in defence, which he did not particularly enjoy but he had put the team first. This left the coach's award, which we both knew had to go to another midfielder who had been sensational all year, one of the bravest players I have ever seen play and the best attitude any manager could hope for from a player. He had also come second and third in the players' and parents' awards. But the coach would not have it; he insisted his son had to win an award. His son had also been good, but the lad who missed out had been phenomenal and was the ultimate team player, which was a massive factor in all the awards.

The best he could offer me was for me to give the other lad the players' or parents' award, as he came second and third in the two, rather than both to the captain – basically lie about the votes. I was happy to use discretion to ensure more boys got awards, but I was not prepared to manipulate an actual vote where a player had won it fairly and lie to the players or parents about the voting numbers. He stuck to his guns, though, and gave his award to his son. I still feel bad for the lad who missed out, although I am good mates with his dad and they both know what happened.

Even once he was manager, long after I had stepped down, his nonsense continued at the expense of the team. A local company who had kindly sponsored the team previously contacted me and offered to buy tracksuits for the squad. I texted the coach regarding the very generous offer to put him in touch with the sponsor, only to be told, "Boys are not having tracksuits this season." I thought he misunderstood and explained they were completely free; it was effectively a gift to the team (worth the best part of a grand) and would not cost the players or parents a penny. But it was no good; he did understand but as ever was happy to let the boys miss out on something nice because presumably the offer had come through me. I know for a fact he did not even ask the players if they wanted the tracksuits; it was typically petty.

I look back now, and I get it to a point. I can see how it would have been a blow to his ego seeing 'his team' managed differently and doing well after they had folded under him previously. He had pressure from his son and wife, who also were used to him being in charge and really did not like things being done differently, but there was no excuse for the constant backstabbing and dishonesty, both to me and the parents and players. It was completely unacceptable, especially as I had given him and his son a chance when his last three teams had folded in successive years.

However, I was warned and really, how can I complain when he was dishonest in joining us, going behind his manager's back, within the same club. Not to mention warnings from when he was the manager. It was not difficult to see why his teams had always folded and why he would have an issue with me. It was much harder to accept his behaviour towards my players and parents; the constant deceit was very tiresome.

For anyone going into junior football management, choose who you work with carefully and take heed of warning signs. It is unlikely to be a coincidence when every team a coach is involved in, ends up folding! Not everyone is involved for the right reasons. Football (even junior football) can be a very murky world.

A Junior Football Manager

VILE PARENT

It had been a good game between two well-matched teams played in good spirits by the children. Unfortunately, the game was being spoilt by a group of parents from the home team, which was also the club I had played for and had refereed for in various games across several age groups since I'd stopped playing.

Every decision I made for the away team was met by foul-mouthed abuse from one particular dad. I asked the parent directly to stop the abuse or the game could not continue and asked the manager to ensure this happened. A few minutes later, I gave a foul to the away team for a very clear and obvious foul by a home team player.

The parent screamed from the other side of the pitch in full earshot of all the players and parents calling me a 'fucking cunt'. I stopped the game again and told him and the other parents that I was sending him off and the game would be abandoned if the parent did not leave the pitch. After further similar abuse, the team's manager finally persuaded him to leave the pitch and go to the car park.

He was still walking towards the car park when I restarted the game and the home team scored almost immediately. Realising they had scored, the parent screamed from a distance, again in full earshot of the children and parents, "Have some of that, you cunt."

This was an under-nines friendly, not even a competitive match. Most of the children were eight years old.

An Eighteen-year-old Junior Football Referee

MY WORST PERFORMANCE

We were 5-0 down at home to a very good side in the league, only a couple of minutes to go by my watch, when our winger went down under a crunching tackle. We got the free kick, but he stayed down. I got the nod from the referee to come on, so I made my way over to the far side of the pitch, where our player was still down. I was directly in front of some of their parents and our parents were roughly ten yards from the halfway line. I spoke to our player, and he had taken a bang on his ankle, nothing serious, and got up pretty quickly after moving his foot around. The referee then asked me to take him off the pitch and walk along to the halfway line and wait for his signal to come back on (that was the rule).

I walked the player up the line to wait for the referee's signal; as I approached the halfway line there was a group of dads from the away team standing there. As I approached them, I was greeted with, "Your team's a joke." I kept quiet, my player got the nod to go back on, then the same guy repeated, "Your team's a joke and you're a joke." This was my first mistake. I should have just walked away and not given him the time of day, but I turned around to look at the fella who said it. He is in a group of about five so obviously feeling very brave and pleased with himself; he said it again: "You're a joke and so is your team."

I straight away recognised this guy from the first game we'd played against them at their ground earlier on in the season. They were an excellent team, and we were not expected to get any kind of result against them. Their manager was a really nice young coach associated with a professional club. Always calm and I had a lot of respect for him in the way he ran his team. The first game finished 0-0; they had a goal ruled out for offside which could have been deemed harsh, but the referee had the final say and he gave the offside. Well, this did not go down well with some of their parents, especially the guy who thought my team and I were a joke. He was their linesman that day and after that decision he decided to flag our forward offside for just walking towards their goal. Was I happy? No, of course not, but was happy with the result, picking up a point away against a very good team.

Anyway, once I turned to this guy he decided to step forward. My parents, who were ten yards or so away, started to shuffle down the line away from me, all apart from my wife, that is, who could see me standing there with five other guys in front of me. She came over and stood next to me to say ignore it; I smiled and just stood there. This was my second mistake; I should have moved away from them. They started laughing and my wife asked, "What's so funny? Do you think it's funny laughing at twelve- to thirteen-year-olds getting hurt on a football pitch and encouraging your players to get stuck in to our players?"

At this point he leaned right in towards her face. This guy was my size, six foot one, maybe two, and he was leaning in to try and intimidate my wife, who is five foot one – wow, what a powerful guy he must feel right now. As he leaned in, he said, "I can laugh at whoever and whatever I want." When

I saw this, I immediately tried to grab the man away from my wife; this was the third and biggest mistake I made. One of the other parents managed to pull him out of the way before I actually touched him; in hindsight this was a good thing as it could have escalated a lot worse than it did.

At the point I tried to grab the man the referee turned to see just that; he blew his whistle and made his way over. All he saw was me going for the parent, nothing of what had led up to it; it could not have looked good. The referee blew his whistle to signal the end of the game. I was fuming as I walked away to the other side of the pitch, not with the result but with what I had just got myself involved in.

What gives a forty-odd-year-old man the right to laugh at a child who is hurt, cheers when they get hurt, encourage their own team to hurt other players on the pitch and try to intimidate a woman? All I can say is, he must be missing something in his life; if he carried on like that in any other walk of life, he would not get away with it for too long, but on the side of a football pitch this is seen as acceptable. So the referee blew up, ended the game a minute or so early, although on my watch we must have been well into injury time.

I went home and tried to digest what had just happened at the match, still fuming with myself for getting involved, but it was done, and I would learn from it. Or so I thought.

In the next few days, I got a call from our club chairman telling me the referee's report had not painted me in a good light, along the lines of saying I had tried to grab the parent. OK, yes, I did, that is true, anything else? I am first to admit when I am wrong and I was definitely in the wrong, but I wasn't the only one. The chairman asked for the whole story; like an idiot I was expecting some sort of back-up. Instead I was met with, "Why was your wife getting involved?" "You can't act like that as a coach." "You have to lead by example." I knew all of this, but had this happened anywhere else other than a football match the outcome would have been very different. My chairman said that this would be going to the FA and to expect a fine. I asked about the parent from the other team, and he said nothing was mentioned apart from my actions. I was gutted; this parent had started it all and nothing was being done about his behaviour; he was everything wrong in a parent on the side-lines at kids' football.

When I next saw our chairman, he said the league had mentioned about a possible points deduction and awarding the game to the other team. "What?" I said. "They won the game 5-0 – they have the points." But he was obviously talking about a further three points being taken away. My heart sank; I felt sick. "They can't do that, not to the lads, it's me who has fucked up, not them." If they deducted the points I would have to step down as manager; I wouldn't be able to look any of them in the eye or their parents. "I've let everyone down, it's me who should be punished, give me a fine, even a ban, I don't care, but don't take three points off the team. If they take points off us, I will take it further, go to the FA and appeal, the team do not deserve that."

I asked again, "Is anything happening about the other parent's actions?"

The reply was, "Nothing at all."

I had to wait a further few weeks before the chairman called with the outcome; the call went along the lines of:

Chairman: "Hi, mate, how are you?"

Myself: "OK, thanks. You?"

C: "Right, what the hell happened that day?"

M: "What do you mean? I told you what happened. Please don't tell me we have a points deduction."

C: "No, but you got a fine, and a big fine – that's why I ask again, what happened? It's a bigger fine than the club has ever had before."

At this point I'm relieved at the team not getting points deducted but also nervous at what the biggest fine in the club's history is.

M: "OK, how big are we talking?"

C: "£80, the biggest fine to date."

M: "OK, so how do I appeal this fine?"

C: "I wouldn't bother if I were you as it could get worse. Pay the fine and let that be the end of it."

M: "OK, and still nothing from the parent who was mocking our players and squared up to my wife?"

C: "No, nothing, it is best to let it go."

I think the club's biggest fine before my fine was around £50 – nothing I am proud of whatsoever, but it was made out to be worse than it actually was. Don't get me wrong, it's still a good amount of money, but in my head, I was thinking a lot more by the way he was speaking.

We waffled some more on the phone before the call ended. When I hung up it was mixed emotions that I was feeling. First relief at not costing the team a three-point deduction because of my stupidity, second was also relief at not getting some kind of suspension, but third I was angry that I had been made an example of because of my position as a manager. Yes, I didn't cover myself in glory that day, but the parent/parents who goaded me, laughed at injured kids and mocked a group of twelve- to thirteen-year-olds did not even get a slap on the wrist about their behaviour.

It was a lesson learnt on my behalf, but could the same be said for the parent/parents that day? The answer is no. I know this because we knew some parents from the team and they said that particular parent was a nightmare most weeks; it is pathetic that any father would think this behaviour was acceptable, let alone in front of kids. What was being done to stop this guy? Why was his team and club allowing this to happen every week? As coaches/managers we have to lead by example, but as a parent you also have a duty to behave on the other side of a kids' football pitch and respect the environment they are in.

It makes you wonder, is this guy acting like this walking down the street? Does he act like this at home around his family and friends? I am pretty sure he doesn't, so why at a kids' football game is it the only acceptable environment for this behaviour? We all have daily struggles and stresses to deal with, but coming to watch your child should not be stressful or a struggle; it should be enjoyable. Yes, we want our child to be good at football, but let them enjoy it. I cannot think of any other sport where this is tolerated, but for some reason it seems to be acceptable at kids' football, and that is a very sad thing to accept.

A Junior Football Manager

PSYCHOPATH DAD

Both sets of players had behaved well with no real problems. The home parents had been noisy throughout the game, moaning at any decision not going their way. With the score at 2-2 with less than two minutes to play, a home player went down in the penalty box from a fair tackle, so I waved play on.

Some of the players half-heartedly shouted for a penalty; I heard the parents shouting as well, but they were at the other end of the pitch, so I did not hear exactly what was said. I found out afterwards that one particularly loud parent, a fat middle-aged man, had taken great offence at the penalty not being given.

A minute later the away team scored the winner, which was the last straw for him. A short time after, I ended the match and, still oblivious to this man's fury, I collected my stuff and started walking to the car park, where I was getting a lift home from my mum. As I walked closer to the car park, the same man, who had gone back to his car to get an iron bar from the boot, was walking towards me with the bar screaming at how he was going to 'get me back'. Fortunately, some parents of the away team were also walking back with me and bundled him to the floor and enabled me to escape.

I did not carry on refereeing for long after this and many other incidents.

A Junior Football Referee – Aged Fourteen,
Refereeing an Under-twelves Match

REFEREE ASSAULTED

It was a very one-sided game; the home team were much stronger and were several goals up halfway through the second half. The away team had resorted to kicking the home team all over the pitch. Dangerous tackles were flying in; they were very aggressive.

After one particularly horrendous late tackle I booked one of their players, who walked directly towards me and shoulder-barged me when running off. I called him back and sent him off. As I was making a note of the player who had been sent off, I suddenly felt a blow to my throat and sudden pain. I could not breathe for a few seconds and was in complete shock. The player I had sent off had elbowed me in the throat as he'd walked off the pitch. As he walked off his teammates were fist-bumping him.

I was still shaken up and allowed the game to carry on, but shortly before the end I had to send off another player for another assault on an opposition player. The player I sent off approached me and screamed in my face, "Ref, you are a cunt, you have sent me and my brother off."

As soon as I ended the game, I left quickly and did not even collect my match fee.

A Junior Football Referee – Aged Seventeen,
Refereeing an Under-eighteen Game

TOO MUCH POLITICS AND TOO MANY MEETINGS

The craziness started again a few weeks later after what seemed like a very short break. Fresh from the success of winning the league the season before, we were ready for another great season. Confidence was high; in preseason we looked fantastic, going unbeaten in five or six games. I thought we would win the league; despite going up three divisions we were beating everyone; everything looked great. Parents were behaving; it was happy days. Dare I say it, I was even starting to enjoy this football-manager business.

But then the season started, and I went straight back down to earth. It was the definition of 'two steps forward and three steps back'. Anything that could go wrong, went wrong; it was rubbish in every way. The politics off the pitch became a constant and unnecessary irritation and the team spirit amongst the players (which I had always been so proud of) was unrecognisable from the season before.

In the season before I had very much kept a low profile within the club; I went to a few meetings which always very focused on the much younger teams. There were dozens of teams in the younger age groups, and I think at the time there were only three teams from under-fourteen upwards. The only time I said anything, or our team was mentioned, was when we won the league and had the issue with our rivals and the league getting a strong referee in for the title decider following the farce in the first game. I was happy to go now and again, and I was grateful to the club for taking us. I had no problem at all with the focus being on younger age groups and I liked being left to get on with it. I was friendly with one of the club officials and we would have a beer sometimes; I did not know the chairman or the other 'officers' (as they would call themselves).

The club would have a big tournament before the season started. On the pitch we did well, getting to the final of our age group before losing to an EJA team from Ilford. Off the pitch we had been told repeatedly that all managers and coaches were expected to help at the tournament all weekend – from 6am on Saturday setting up to Sunday evening clearing away. Anything from selling drinks and hot dogs to setting up goals, we were told it was expected for us to be there for the duration. I had a slight issue with this as I was self-employed and worked weekends, so for me to help all weekend meant I was actually losing money; it was affecting my livelihood. A few other managers were in the same boat where they worked weekends.

The 'officers' did not agree with this and saw it as much more of a black-and-white issue. Basically, any managers that did not spend all weekend from 6am to the evening on both days were not showing the commitment expected.

I thought it was fairly obvious that someone who had to work all weekend was in a completely different situation to an employed guy who had his weekends off and so was not losing income by giving his time up. Despite this, I got there 6am Saturday and stayed until the evening and came back the next morning; my wife also helped selling raffle tickets and drinks all bloody day. Given my work situation, it was more than generous, and I lost business as a result. There was also the small matter of my having sponsored two teams' kits. The club had done very well out of me, and I was very happy to help but because I didn't do the full Sunday as well, I was told that, I 'was not putting in the commitment', I 'did not care about the club' and 'it's the same people helping all the time'. Completely ignoring the £1,600 in sponsorship money I had provided in order to pay for a couple of sets of kit worth £400 each. A simple thank-you would have been much more appreciated. I was pretty certain selling teas for a day would not have raised anything like the amount I had given to the club; it did seem very short-sighted.

It did concern me that something so simple was seemingly not understood by the chairman of the club and other officers; it was just counting. It was a very strange time all round and the politics really took off; it was vastly different to the season before, or it could have been that I just hadn't really noticed it before. They became obsessed about the meetings which were of little relevance to my team as all the officers were managers of the younger teams.

The most frustrating thing of all was that they had failed to have the one eleven-a-side pitch ready for the season, as it was covered with stones, which was obviously a health hazard.

Their solution was to tell us we were to use training sessions as a 'stone-picking' exercise which consisted of being on your hands and knees picking stones out of a football pitch. I was all for the community spirit on most things and I appreciated the subs charged to parents was cheap, but at the very least they should have had a safe pitch to play on, without having to pick hundreds of stones out of a pitch which made little difference. My fifteen-year-olds were not going to agree to do that or the parents. Again, their reluctance to recognise the difference in age groups became an issue. It was different to the under-sixes and -sevens, where you could sell it to them as some kind of 'adventure'. They did not really seem to see the actual football as important; it more had the feel of a youth or community club with football almost an irrelevance.

Although I did not agree with the way it was being run, I had a lot of time for the club and liked everyone personally, and I thought they did care for the children's welfare. I had come from a club where winning was everything and the children's welfare was ignored. But this was the other extreme, where winning and the actual football did not matter at all, and everything was much more focused on non-football issues and much younger children. As the oldest age group, we were in a very different place to children still at primary school, so the same approach would not work. Fifteen-year-olds want to win, they want to take it seriously, they don't always agree with the 'it's the taking part that counts' and they certainly will not go to football training to pick stones up. I backed them on this; the one thing a football team has to have is a pitch to play – it's the one thing you cannot really do without!

It was still a good place to be, and where I was friendly with the guy that sorted out the pitches and kick-off times, I was able to pretty much go with the flow and get good kick-off times and usually get to my younger son's games (especially if we were both at home). Other managers who did not have as good a relationship with the pitch guy got stitched up every week. Afternoon kick-offs, crappy pitches. It was wrong, really, very political, but at the time it suited me, so I was not going to argue. There was one time when one of the managers after a few shandies one evening and after another rubbish kick-off time and venue allocated, did a group email to all the managers and officers asking why the same managers got looked after and the same manager got stitched up all the time, suggesting a little favouritism. The club did not like that one bit; it was true, though.

All managers were supposed to be Level 1 qualified, which to the untrained ear sounds pretty impressive. Think again: the Level 1 course is impossible to fail; it has a 100% pass rate so perhaps is not so impressive. Ironically, I was one of the few managers in the club to never get the badge; I did the 'safeguarding' part and the first weekend, but I turned my ankle in the practical, which was very embarrassing at the time, and could hardly walk for a week so did not go back for the second weekend. I was going to rebook but then found out it was largely meaningless – what sort of 'qualification' has a 100% pass rate! I did my own silent protest and swerved it.

At my previous club, United, one manager had been scheduled to go to a Level 1 course but was unable to attend. In classic FA style, they sent the club the certificate to say he had passed despite not turning up! The club was more than happy to turn a blind eye to the error and mark him as 'qualified', which really says everything you need to know about that qualification.

The off-the-field politics and frustrations were nothing compared to the nightmare I was having with the team on the pitch. We had a few new faces who were decent players, but they did not settle, and it seemed to upset the mix and morale of the team. The squad was also now too big, causing all sorts of problems with game time, and these boys were growing up, hormones and egos were flying around, and I found it much harder to connect with them. They were not kids anymore but also were not adults – far from it!

The season before had been so good and creating the team spirit we'd had was the biggest achievement of all. Sadly, the same team spirit seemed to disappear very quickly. Social media became an issue within the team, and it got quite nasty with the boys setting up online groups which excluded a few of the players, creating cliques and division within the squad. I would get complaints from parents about things boys had put on their 'group chat', really offensive stuff against other boys – bullying, basically. They would then have group chats within group chats so two or three boys would not be included. I was then becoming involved in issues completely unrelated to football; it was a nightmare from start to finish.

I had never had an issue dealing with a kid who was noisy or even aggressive and generally a pain-in-the-arse teenager – we have all been there; teenagers are meant to be stroppy! I always thought I was good at dealing with the kids and their various issues, but I realised I was not good at dealing with the more subtle, sneaky behaviours. A little word here and there, lads manipulating other lads and causing division, and the online aspect of it all drove me round the bend. I just didn't know how to deal with it.

We actually we won our first game of the season then in our second game played our old friends from United, a couple of months on since the 6-0 thrashing. I don't think I have seen a worse game than on that day. All of the good form and goals dried up overnight; we were awful. And by half time we were unrecognisable to the team we had been for a year. Players screaming at each other and slagging each other off, no passing, no teamwork; we could have played all day and would not have scored. I have to admit United played a good game; they dealt with our attacking threats and frustrated the life out of us. No doubt they were super-charged after the 6-0 defeat, not wanting to be embarrassed again and completely stopped us playing. We had never been in that position; we had always been the team to stop the other team playing, the underdogs.

It ended 0-0 and it was as if we had lost 10-0. I have never understood what happened that day; it was like a dark cloud covering us all. We looked completely deflated and depressed. United were the opposite, well pleased to get a point against us, which I thought was a positive and showed how far we had come; we had only been a team for a year. We were still unbeaten in a year, top of the league after a couple of games: a win and a draw. I have never seen an overreaction like it; it really was not that bad, but something changed. The team spirit you could already see was different to the previous season.

The next game was in the cup against the team that ended

up winning the division, a really tough game. It was horrible, with cheating parents and managers deciding the game, and it was also one of only two games ever that I could not attend. There was no referee allocated, which meant the two teams had to referee themselves. Bob took the first half and one of their guys did the second half. Bob was subjected to abuse from their players, their manager and their parents for every minute of that first half; the team was vile. The game was delicately balanced at 1-1 with ten minutes left. Their striker was played through but was at least two yards offside, so our linesman (one of our parents) immediately flagged. The referee, however, ignored the flag and 'overruled' the offside. It was not even close; obviously there was uproar. The 'referee' told our linesman to 'fuck off' when he told him again it was offside. I wish I had been there; I would have taken all the boys off the pitch; it was disgusting.

Knocked out of the cup, first loss in a year without genuinely losing. I felt for the boys; again football ruined by adults. What sort of example did it set? Cheating does work. To really rub salt into the wounds, the 'referee', who was the brother of one the players, had in the previously season let a cup game go on for ten minutes extra (despite no injuries) until his team had scored, which had been reported to the league. I reported it to the league, but of course nothing was done, and he was able to carry on reffing. It was embarrassing; I was all for winning and going all out, but that was shameful. We ended up losing more matches than we won and generally bickering and having dramas most weeks; it was all quite depressing.

I tried everything to turn it around. We continued to do

things outside of football: I set up some social events and organised some training at the boxing club, all of which had worked so well the previous season. It wasn't the same; some boys would mysteriously come down with illness or injury before the fitness training (but be fine for school and for the match at weekend) or simply slag it off – "What's boxing got to do with football?" – which was ridiculous as fitness and strength was the biggest factor at the level we were playing, especially as now boys were bigger and more aggressive. Everything was so negative; this was definitely going to be my last season.

The coaching set-up also did not work, which contributed to the problems. There were now three of us, which was too many; invariably we would have different ideas and sometimes mixed messages would go out to the players, which is a pet hate for me and yet we were now doing it. I felt as if the team was not really mine anymore; I made all the wrong calls and do feel I let some of the lads down a bit.

In what was one of the most unpleasant games I have ever been part of, we played a local team who had a point to prove, as a couple of our new players had played for them, as well as some other lads who used to play for the local rivals United. We had played them the week before in another nightmare game in a cup which we had won 2-1; this time was at their ground. One lad was the angriest kid I have ever seen in football; I thought he was on drugs. He was literally frothing at the mouth from the first second. He screamed abuse at our players, me and even our parents (when they objected to his fourth foul that should have been a yellow card). The referee (who was openly being called a cunt by parents and players) was appalling; he was petrified of them. I asked him outright at the end of the match why he had not sent the player off for any one of the dozen offences and he could not give a reason other than looking in the direction of the parents.

They went 2-0 up and I wished the game could have ended there; it was horrible. At one point my assistant ran to get the ball and they kicked it out of his hands as he went to grab it, all of their parents finding it hilarious. I then ran and got a ball that the goalkeeper was not even attempting to retrieve to take a goal kick and of course got absolutely slaughtered by the parents. The lowest point (which was saying something) was their 'linesman', one of their parents. Every single ball forward he was flagging offside; the referee knew he was cheating but had bottled the game completely. I went directly behind him for a few minutes to be absolutely sure and of course another ball played into their half, our striker had to be three yards behind two of their defenders and he did it again. I did not help the situation by truthfully calling him a disgrace.

We actually got a goal back and I was desperate to get a draw to shut everyone up, but they held on, and you would of thought they had won the premiership. In one game, every single thing that was wrong with junior football. Abusive parents, cheating parent/linesman, a petrified and abused referee too scared to make the correct decisions and terribly behaved kids (not really surprising given the madness around them).

I was on the verge of giving up there and then, I was so sick of it, but out of loyalty to the boys I decided to call it a day as soon as the season finished. It took an eternity, and we ended a couple of points above the relegation places – maybe we shouldn't have gone up so many divisions. Ironically, the only bright spot was that the last remaining team at United came bottom and folded completely, so I guess we could have been worse. I was gutted because Bob had left with his son after more in-house arguments between players. I tried my best to please everyone, but in the end, I pleased no one! It did not matter about losing matches; it just wasn't enjoyable anymore for anyone.

Then, to my surprise, it became evident that the lads did want to stick together and carry on, and then I started getting texts from new parents and players asking to join. More teams had folded, players wanted to go another season and it started going crazy with interest. None of the existing players wanted to leave (not that you would have known judging by the happiness levels most games that season) and suddenly we had enough interested players to fill two or three teams. Although it had been a pretty awful, I would like to think we had still tried to make it a good place to be and did much more for the kids than most teams. Maybe for the first time ever there was some reward for our efforts over the years.

I spoke to my son, and he suggested that in view of the interest and potential we do it one more season, and my long-suffering younger son, who I had promised to see play every game when I gave up, gave his blessing. So, we agreed to go one more year. I really liked the new players wanting to join; they were good, and a couple had come down from higher divisions, but more importantly they wanted a change and to be part of a whole new challenge, and I liked their personalities, really good characters. Just as importantly, I could see their parents were genuine and I could see would get behind and be part of the team.

We held a trial training session, and I was running late; as I got out the car, there were about thirty lads waiting on the pitch all wanting to join – the word had spread; I could not believe it. So, we realised we could create a second team and a couple of parents very bravely stepped up to manage it. Suddenly, all the negativity of the season had gone; it was exciting, and the football bug was back. It was all about the next season and we now had two teams with thirty under-sixteen boys playing for us, which really was something when we looked back to the bad old days of being a laughing stock and not being able to field a full team, let alone have a full squad.

After the grim season we had, I was determined to do it the right way again. I was not going to allow any politics or other nonsense in. It was going to be the last year: the boys had their GCSEs at the end of it; they were becoming young men. This would be the last season for some and definitely me, I really wanted it to be special for them and maybe even win something. We needed to recreate the team spirit of our first season, and although we were making it up as we went along that season it'd worked: the boys had a wonderful time and I wanted that again.

The main thing I did change was accept that the boys were now young adults, not children. I let them choose how they wanted to approach the season and team. The club was a massive advocate of winning not mattering and taking part being everything, which I agreed with in the young teams, which made up most of the club. But sixteen-year-olds full of ego and testosterone did not agree with this in a million years. They wanted to go for it and try to win; their enjoyment was the winning, not so much the taking part. So we all agreed to take it seriously – no not turning up at training or messing around. Most importantly to keep the egos to a minimum, putting the team first, not individuals. It was a big ask!

SC

DO YOU KNOW THAT WE ARE VOLUNTEERS

"Do you know I am a volunteer?"

"Do you know that I am giving up my own time?"

"Do you know I don't get paid for this?"

"If you don't like it, you can do my job."

Every junior manager has said something similar to the statements and questions above. Often when telling off kids who are taking the piss and misbehaving whilst you are trying to teach them something. We did it on occasion; after all, it is correct: we are all volunteers and do give up our own time for free.

But has there ever been a more overused sentiment or phrase in junior football? I doubt it. I knew other managers and club officials who used it on an hourly basis. If a club meeting went more than five minutes without those classic words or similar, it was a shock. I don't think I ever had a conversation with a club or league without being quoted the dreaded phrase or a variation of it.

The problem is that as soon as the 'volunteer' part comes

out, it excuses all further actions and behaviours, irrespective of how incompetent and poor they are. It is effectively a licence to have an unwarranted sense of self-righteousness and superiority for as long as you are a 'volunteer' over any criticism or challenge that comes your way.

We never agreed with this culture. Of course, anyone who steps up as a manager, a chairman, a club official/officer or a league official deserves respect, as they are enabling our children to play football. And parents should always show respect to managers who are giving hundreds of hours of their time every year for their son. But people in all of the above roles who have volunteered can still be useless and sometimes can do it for all the wrong reasons, nothing to do with wanting our children to play football safety. I have been told several times over the years, "If you don't like it, you can do my job," when raising even the most innocuous question or concern regarding child welfare. Even when someone is categorically in the wrong the old 'volunteer' and 'if you don't like it' phrases are brought out.

As with anything in life, some of the people that volunteer to help leagues and clubs are great, probably the majority. But some are not great and do it as a power trip or because they want to play the martyr, forever moaning about how much they hate doing the job whilst doing it badly year after year. Why volunteer to do something if you are going to begrudge it every day? Life is too short surely. Do it for the right reasons and not for a constant pat on the back, and definitely don't throw out the 'do you know I'm a volunteer?' at every opportunity.

Some of the league and club officials I had to deal with at

different times were seriously hard work. The email signature below is an actual word-for-word title used in emails by an old club official at one of the clubs we played under:

Name ____
Club Secretary
Girls' manager and coach just for the love of it.
Under-tens manager and coach for the love of it.
Under-twelves manager, part-time coach for the love of it, a true unpaid volunteer.

Just in case you missed it, he really loves helping the club and kids and clearly does not do it for any other reason or mention it much!

These are some of our personal experiences over the years in dealing with clubs, leagues, referees and other managers.

I got on with most of the managers from our club; I did not always agree with what they were saying or doing but respected their opinion. Some of the committee members I couldn't say the same about; some used it to really benefit the team they were running. I remember on one occasion the committee member/manager who was paid to cut the grass at our training facility had only cut the area his team trained in, so most of the other age groups, including ours, had to train in long grass that day. Club officials would always get the new equipment, pick of pitches and training times.

I was asked to be a committee member with the joint title of vice chairman along with another guy. I thought, *Great, finally I will be able to have an input into the behind-the-scenes running of the club.* How wrong I was. Pretty much everything I said fell on deaf ears and that was when I really began to see that people were doing it for their own benefit. I lasted a few months and would move my team to another club after the season was finished as I didn't want to be involved with lining the chairman's pockets.

You meet many different managers and coaches over the seasons. The majority are in the same boat as you: they care for their team and share the same frustrations with parents, leagues and clubs, and you get on really well. You come across many characters, and everyone has their own style. Occasionally some managers were rude and could not even muster a hello when you were exchanging your cards and forms. Some just loved to chat when all you wanted to do was get lads warmed up. You would always get a manager now and again who would say, "We have had some injuries this season, my striker is missing and my best player is ill," trying to make excuses as to why they might not win the match. Probably 75% were nice guys trying their best to get kids playing football every week in the same way you would be. The other 25% were everything that is wrong in junior football, setting a terrible example to their players. Turning up late, screaming at their players non-stop for ninety minutes and giving abuse to the referee and linesman every single match.

Managers can also be the most stubborn people in the world. I have seen teams come bottom of the league, barely win a game season after season, but maintain 'X is a defender, not a midfielder', 'Y is not suited at the back' or 'Z is a natural striker', ignoring the fact that the defence and attack was the worst in league. What is there to lose by giving kids the chance to experience different positions? If it doesn't work out nothing will change, and the team can carry on losing! If you are losing every week anyway, why not let kids experience different positions? Every manager will have a different view, and in fairness, however bizarre decisions may seem to players or parents, they are doing their best. I am sure we were exactly the same, and parents and players all thought they knew better. Football divides opinions like nothing else and junior football is no exception: everyone thinks they know best; it is completely normal. The biggest criticism of other teams' managers I had was their inability to deal with problem parents. I appreciate it is not always easy to deal with an aggressive guy, especially when you have more than enough on your plate on a match day, but I would never have allowed a parent to behave half as badly as we would regularly witness.

One manager's team had just been promoted to the premier league and contacted me for a friendly, so we arranged the match. For me preseason friendlies were not about the results but getting the fitness levels up and trying new things as well as new players sometimes. So this manager was confident; his team had won the first division convincingly so were full of confidence. When we met over at their ground, I remember meeting him and shaking hands with him, then he started to say to me he wanted friendlies with mediocre prem teams. He clearly classed us as 'mediocre', which was fine; it was his opinion. He was also going on about how good his striker was and how he would bag a load of goals in the coming season. I wished him good luck and went over to sort my team out.

The game got underway, and we started slowly, and

within ten minutes they scored and celebrated wildly. As their manager walked past me, he smugly said to me, "Welcome to the premier league." I must admit I wanted to bite but just sniggered instead. He shouted and screamed all game; even his lads were mouthy, telling myself and our coach we were shit. It all changed when we started to get a grip of the game and ended up winning 8-2. Their team was not used to being beat so heavily and started to try and kick lumps out of our lads, and it spilled over a few times – so much for a friendly. After the game I went over to their manager with a smirk on my face and wished him good luck in the prem. That season they finished bottom without winning a game and barely scoring any goals.

There is nothing worse than managers who would actively 'tap up' players from other teams. This goes on far too much; it goes back to adults ruining the game for the children. It is not the Premier League – if a team and a child is happy, why not let him be? I had a lad who went to play for another team because the manager said his parents could use his holiday home abroad if he joined.

My son's old manager used to drive me insane with his views on football and team selections; he had his view and wild horses would not change it. Win, lose or draw, the same players played the same positions every time. I don't think we ever agreed on anything to do with football, whether it was the Premiership and West Ham or the kids playing junior football. But he was a great guy and cared for his players, and as ever football is all about opinions; there is no 'right way'. We are still friends now and still disagree with anything to do with football!

On the other end of the spectrum my son's last manager was one of the few managers I've ever met who was a complete wrong 'un. He was one of those guys whose every other sentence was 'it's all about the kids', which could not have been further from the truth. He was petrified of a few parents and would bow down to whatever they wanted. I was at a training session once when a parent decided the drills he was doing with the kids were crap and literally interrupted it to take over, telling the manager to take a break. At first, I felt sorry for him, it must have been very undermining, but he would take out his frustrations at being mugged off by the parents on some of the players without such dominant parents, knowing they would not kick off if they were dropped or played out of position.

He dropped one boy from the squad completely by text. The boy's mum screenshot a copy of the text conversation and put it on the group chat; it was horrible and really highlighted the complete hypocrisy as he was still telling anyone who would listen 'it's all about the kids'. The parents he was desperate to impress could not care less about him; he was just useful to them, giving countless lifts to training and the guarantee of starting their son in every game. Watching him giving out end-of-season awards without a single parent or player giving him a card or a gift was so awkward. Especially when the other teams in the club were all getting their managers cards and prezzies. In in the first year, I actually did buy him a box of beers because I felt so bad for him.

By the second season I could see exactly the man he was. He made a big point of telling everyone that he 'would pick the team based on form' and if you played well you 'would keep the shirt'; he was always a walking cliche. My son came off the bench two games in a row, played really well, helped turn a losing position to a win or a draw but still started sub the next games. When I politely asked him why he was not following his own self-made policy, he dug deeper by telling me that my son had told him he had an injury and he had not started him as a precaution! My son had not said anything of the sort to him in either game. He did seem to be a compulsive liar; he would often get caught out saying different things to different people, not realising parents and players talk. It was all very odd.

We often found there were too many middle-aged men playing politics and having power trips; it was not about kids playing football at all. Some of the club officials did not even like football; they had never played and had no interest in watching games. The perception they had of players was often completely out of touch with the reality; it was something they read from an FA textbook. The constant messages of 'it's not about winning' and 'it's about the boys enjoying themselves' with no awareness at all that boys want to win. Winning is the bit they enjoy, especially once they get to their teenage years. They never even tried to speak to the kids and ask them how they felt; they would just talk to each other and tell the kids how they felt. These messages would then be contradicted completely by most of the managers of teams within the club, who would be screaming and shouting on a Sunday, desperate for their team to win the match and treating it like the World Cup final. There was never any middle ground and common sense shown.

The whole 'it's all about winning' versus 'it's not about winning but all about taking part' will always be debated. The correct position is probably somewhere between these two extremes. We all like to win; football fans/players/managers/parents want to win more than anyone. Just look at the reaction when your team scores a goal at any level in any league, including in children's football. It is absurd for the FA or football clubs to say that winning does not matter. I used to cringe when I heard, far too often, the words 'the boys have to learn life is not about winning' and 'they need to learn to lose'. This was something I heard from parents as well as clubs. I thought it was the completely wrong message to give young people. Why can they not try to win, and work together to improve? You might end up losing but at least you gave it a go, which deserves massive credit. Even better, you might just win something, and what better preparation for life than a real-life example of the good things that can happen with some hard work and commitment? Either way, telling the kids that they are going to lose, and life is about losing, so get used to it, I could never get my head round.

At the younger ages, the FA have it right; they are very much still kids and all that should matter is them playing football and enjoying it. But again, leagues and clubs don't actually enforce these messages with any sincerity – do all the managers and parents buy into that philosophy? Absolutely not, you still get all the nonsense: parents abusing referees and managers, desperate to win at all costs, lambasting children for doing something wrong on the football pitch when they are not even in secondary school. The constant mixed messages are not fair on the children.

The hypocrisy of the club officials who were also managers within a club was something to behold; they would lecture managers on how 'their way' of managing was the blueprint for everyone whilst setting all the wrong examples. Definitely a case of 'do what I say, not what I do', judging by the ranting, raving and man-child strops I saw several times.

My younger son was playing in a game against the other team in the same age group within the same club; the other team was managed by the club chairman. For a year I heard about how coaching should be done and kids should be managed at the meetings, so I was looking forward to seeing this magic in real life. They had beaten my son's team 5-0 in the previous league match, so we definitely had a score to settle.

It was a really good game and my son's team played really well; they deservedly scored, and it was 1-0 at half time. I had not seen anything out of the ordinary from Mr Chairman apart from him acting like a typical manager, probably shouting too much. As the tension grew and we still held on to the lead you could see he was getting more stressed and vocal by the minute. Then, with about twenty minutes to go, his son the goalkeeper was about to take a goal kick. Suddenly Mr Chairman ran onto the pitch, holding up the game completely in order to approach his son and clearly berate him for something he must have said or done. Managers are not allowed on the pitch full stop and certainly not to 'tell off' your son.

It must have been horrible for the lad, and any other team could have really kicked up a fuss, but I guess against another team in same club when you are the chairman, who can stop you? We held on to win 1-0 and the boys were well pleased. The chairman's team was not so happy; they were fed up and wanted to go home. It had not been their day. It was a freezing January morning, they had just lost, they just wanted to see their parents and go home to the warmth. Mr Chairman kept them behind after the game for a good twenty minutes; he was still lecturing them by the time we had our managers' post-match debrief, packed everything away and driven off. They were just kids; it was uncalled for. They did not lose deliberately, so he should have had his post-mortem at training the following week. It was not the FA Cup final; it was two mid-division teams in the fourth division of a local league. If that was the right way to do things, I was very content in continuing to do it the 'wrong way'.

On another occasion, I was able to see the second half of one of my son's games after we had played. They were playing a friendly against the team in the age group above, so under-thirteens vs under-fourteens. It was a ridiculous match to arrange; there is a big size difference at those ages, so it was not fair or safe. Not to mention it was never going to end well, as the older age group were in a lose-lose situation. If they did not win it would be highly embarrassing for the kids playing, especially at that age. And if they won, it was meaningless as they were playing the age group below.

The older team was managed by a club official, and he clearly had no such reservations. It was evident from talking to our parents at half time that he was going all out to win and was also refereeing the game. I was told we had gone a couple of goals up which the other team and him did not like one bit. Late tackles, constant aggression and all of it ignored by the manager/referee/club official. In the second half I saw for myself: it was awful; he was letting his own team bully and kick kids a year younger in order to win the game. They ended up winning by a couple of goals. Must have been a proud moment, struggling to beat a team half your size whilst cheating. I looked his team up after; they were poor and had struggled to win any games the season before, which I guess explained his approach and conduct. For it to happen within the club in a match that would not have even been legal in the league, involving a manager who was a club official, spoke volumes. I raised my concerns later with the club through another club official, who told me that all the other club 'officers' knew he was useless, and it was not worth complaining as nothing would come of it as he did the club's finances so was useful to them.

The Child Welfare Officer (CWO) always sounded a good title and role. Sadly, I never really saw them do anything to ensure the children's welfare. The best example of the complete apathy shown to any concerns ever raised I witnessed was when I asked for the CWO to attend one of our matches as we expected the other team to be very aggressive as there had been problems in previous games; we had already made a complaint to the league, who as ever were taking months to respond. He did not want to attend, and his brilliant advice was:

"My advice would be whilst the above incidents are investigated, if you in any way feel the players are at risk by playing against a particular team then don't

play the game as their welfare is far more important than three points!"

He just did not get it; his response to threats and intimidation in junior football as a child welfare officer was to not play! We were trying to win the league; my players would have refused to not play. How is that any solution? To turn a blind eye again to appalling behaviour in junior football, to not even try and push back and improve things for the children's welfare. Sadly, this was far too common; as soon as there was an actual issue threatening children's welfare the clubs and leagues would go AWOL. They took it seriously on their website, though, and had all sorts of nice words telling everyone how seriously they took child welfare.

Referees were like the managers: some were doing it for the good of the sport, some just for the money and some for the power trip. "This wouldn't go ahead if it wasn't for people like me," was what one referee said to me. Well, he was kind of right, but he wouldn't be doing it if there were no teams to referee, so we all needed each other. For me, a good referee makes a decision without hesitation and stands by it, but of course, like anyone, will make mistakes. It is a thankless task, and they suffer constant abuse for not much money, although at least it softens the blow. One referee told me he did at least two games every weekend and it paid for his summer holiday – fair play to him.

One of the worst sights in junior football was when you would turn up and see the referee laughing and joking with the opposing manager, which to me spelt trouble, poor decisions from start to finish and dubious offsides. One time when we drew 0-0 against a lesser team the opposing manager had got his mate to ref the game; he was a qualified ref, but we had to beat them to win the league and he did not want that at all costs. So up stepped his mate and it was the most appalling game I have ever seen by a referee. So we didn't win the league on their patch and after the match their manager took the referee into the club house to buy him a beer. Justice was done the following week when we did win the league.

Referees tended to be one of three types:

1. Decent and strong enough to play it fair without getting intimidated by the parents.
2. Probably decent but terrified of parents so too scared to give decisions against the baying mob.
3. Not decent at all, deliberately and obviously biased, and favouring one team – often mates with the manager of the home team.

My worst memory of a referee was way back when the kids were eleven or twelve. We were getting smashed 6-0 in Southend (as usual). The referee was based at the other team's ground; he was an old boy and knew their manager and all the parents – he seemed to be part of the family. He had already told me off, daring to run on the pitch to look after one of my players who had been kicked. I thought he had waved me on. We got a corner in the last minute of the game; I asked him how long was left, and his exact words were, "This will be the last kick of the game." I put the whole team, apart from the keeper, in the area, desperate for the boys to score. We didn't score from the corner; the keeper caught it, and they quickly went up the other end and scored again, with our boys too knackered to track back. Even at 6-0 up he had to cheat.

Grassroots football does not exist without volunteers; the only people who get paid, as far as I know, are the referees, and who would want to be running around a football pitch for ninety minutes getting a load of abuse for less than thirty pounds? Then again, who would want to be a volunteer involved with grassroots football and doing it all for free? You become a coach, organiser, counsellor, mentor, taxi and parent all in one. Equally, it is not easy running leagues and clubs; anyone stepping into these roles deserves respect. But that is your choice, and just because you are a 'volunteer' in any role in junior football, you still have a responsibility to do the job properly and with integrity. Do it for the right reasons, not for a little power trip or to remind anyone who will listen how virtuous you are. If you feel the need to remind anyone who will listen what a great person you are for being a volunteer, you probably shouldn't be a volunteer.

MJ and SC

THE SUNDAY-MORNING PURGE

Whilst some Sunday mornings going to manage your football team are enjoyable, some really are not. We have mentioned some of the difficulties any junior football manager faces. Problem parents, clueless clubs, incompetent leagues, not to mention the difficulties many teams have in having basic equipment to get a match underway. From balls to kits to nets or even simply a pitch to play on. But for us the biggest problems were parents, not our own parents from our own team but opposing parents who over the years have ruined games repeatedly and in doing so spoilt the kid's experience of playing the game they love. It also ruins the experience of the good parents, many of whom don't abuse the other team's parents, manager, players, linesman and, of course, the match referee – take your pick, it could be all of them in one match.

What can we do about this? Parents screaming at kids from the side-line trying to live their dream through their child. The chances are their child won't make it as a professional footballer, but for some that's hard to accept; if parents looked at the facts, they probably wouldn't fancy their chances much. From a basic internet search it seems there are around 12.7 million children in the UK and roughly 33.3% play football, so just under 4.3 million kids play regularly. The stats say a child will have a less than 0.0001% chance of making it to the Premier League; at the moment of writing this book in the 2021/22 season the Premier League is made up of 41.2% English players, that's 376 players in total out of 915 players registered from ages sixteen to thirty-nine, so that's a rough estimate of sixteen to seventeen English players a season breaking through, less than one per team – that's not good odds!

Often it is not a case of a parent believing their child will make it into the big time. They are just very angry about anything and everything, and the kids' football on a match day is a chance to let out the aggression and frustration. The same guys are probably just as angry when they go to professional matches. At West Ham you see the most normal-looking 'nine to five'-type guy suddenly launch into a hate-filled venomous tirade of abuse over a penalty not given. I used to sit behind a guy who must have been approaching seventy, looked like someone's grandad. He was on his own and every single time the opposing team missed a chance or misplaced a pass, he would leap up and scream abuse along with the 'wanker' hand gesture. This was in front of kids probably the same age as his grandkids – it was not a great look for an OAP.

Just maybe it's the parents who are preventing a bigger percentage of English players actually getting to the heights of the Premier League. By that I mean the aggression and pressure put on some kids while playing football. Let's be honest, we all enjoy doing things we are good at, and we tend to be better at things when we are not under pressure, so why do some parents act the way they do on a Sunday morning when the odds are massively stacked against their child living their parents' dream? Maybe we should change the way the game is watched; we all talk about the way that it's played, but it's the way it's watched and the way the spectators act that actually has a huge effect on any match. In kids' football this really does need to change, but what can we do? We don't have a clue either, but surely someone, somewhere should try to change things. And nice words on club and league websites and Twitter don't count. Some ideas put forward have been:

1. Ban the parents from watching.
2. Parent yellow and red card system.
3. Encourage other parents to speak up.

Banning parents is a simple solution; many sports don't have parents involved and it would make life easier all round for the players, referees and managers. But it is unfair as the (sizable) minority are spoiling it for the majority of parents who can behave and want to support their child. On the plus side children could play in a less pressurised environment, which would improve the confidence and enjoyment of children and even their ability, knowing they wouldn't be being screamed at by parents when they made a mistake. Refereeing would definitely be much fairer, as you would no longer have refs intimidated by one set of parents, meaning the other team don't get a decision all day. Children also wouldn't argue as much with refs, as much of the time they are just copying what they see from the adults. It is not ideal, but until parents can behave, it's the one thing that would at least work.

The problem with 'banning' individual parents is that most grassroots football matches are played in a public playing field, so you can't legally stop anyone from being there. You would hope a parent would respect the decision and stay away, but realistically there's no chance. Some clubs might be lucky enough to have their own private ground – a team we managed did for a short while have its own private land, so maybe it would have worked for us, maybe not. We would have spent most of my time watching out for parents lurking about rather than concentrating on the football; it would just be another thing added to a long list of jobs managers/coaches already have to do.

A parent yellow/red card system would work similar to the players' card system. This would be a job for referees; if they were to feel that they were being abused by a parent or parents from the side-line, or a parent was stepping out of line when it came to abusing a child in some way or another, then the culprit/culprits need to be made accountable. They need to be named and that would mean speaking to the managers at the end of the game to establish who the culprits were and record the yellow card. If at another game the referee has the same problem with this particular person, it would happen again, and two yellows make a red and the parents is banned for three games.

Again, it would be very difficult to manage; some managers might play dumb and claim not to know the problem parent and the parent could well say that if they cannot attend their child cannot play either, which is not fair on the child, but none of this is fair on any child. As a manager you know who the loudmouths are, so it could even be a case that all your parents are on a yellow card so everyone (as well as the mystery parent) would be banned if they misbehave. Harsh? Maybe, but what are we trying to do here? Create a nicer environment for our children to be playing football in or worry about upsetting a loudmouthed thug on the side-line?

Encouraging the parents to speak up could be the most difficult idea of all. Parents will feel threatened themselves if they 'grass' someone up. Managers need to be approachable and make it very clear to all parents that any abusive conduct around the kids is wrong and no one should be doing or turning a blind eye to it. Approaching the manager should be treated as confidential. There were times when a parent was concerned about something that had happened and it was good; they felt they could approach me, so it always got resolved in the correct manner without people either finding out or a drama being created, so this should be the case here.

I know some managers want to be everyone's friend, and all the parents want to be your friend as they feel you will favour their child when it comes to picking the team, but once you stop being manager many of those parents who wanted to have a little chat at every opportunity won't be around. Parents need to be honest themselves as to what they think is acceptable. That a forty-five-year-old man screaming and abusing kids and adults every week would not be allowed to behave this way on the street or anywhere in society. He would be arrested and removed from wherever he was doing it. Why should it be any different just because he is standing in a field with a goal at each end?

The key has to be to clean up the whole game at junior level from the top. The FA and local leagues having a zero-tolerance stance on misconduct and abuse. Changing a culture is very difficult, if not impossible, but it needs to get to the point where it is not seen in any way acceptable for anyone to abuse anyone else at a kids' football match. If a child does it to the referee on the pitch he is sent off; if a parent abuses anyone the club bans him. It can be done; as mentioned earlier at the higher levels where children are in with a realistic chance of making it as a pro, they all behave because the clubs make it very clear their son will be out if they play up. But those parents have an incentive; it is not the same at Sunday-league level.

It is not easy, but clubs and leagues have to step up and take it seriously with much harsher penalties to make everyone realise abuse will not be tolerated. It needs everyone to be 100% engaged and united in working together. FA, leagues, clubs, teams, managers, parents and players all working together. Any notion that swearing and screaming abuse at anyone at a children's football match shows 'passion' has to be dismissed instantly. It's not showing passion to abuse a child or to behave like a thug in front of a child; it is just very sad and cowardly. We gave up reporting anything to the league; our clubs made it very clear it is not worth it as nothing would be done. If you already know the leagues won't do anything it is a further reason to not bother and of course you are back to the volunteer issue. Who needs the hassle when you are not even getting paid? It's easier to turn a blind eye and carry on regardless.

It cannot be beyond the wit of man to make these much-needed changes. It really is time junior football caught up with the rest of society.

MJ and SC

LIKE WATCHING BRAZIL

My last season was very special – one of those rare times in life when everything fits into place and something great happens. I am immensely proud of what those young men achieved and the strength of character they showed; they were magnificent. Helped by a great group of supportive parents (well, the vast majority anyway!), it was a very special time.

We were very happy to have the two teams. Some players moved to the newly formed second team and new players came in for both teams; several players came over from the last United team and another local team that had also folded. There were new faces all round but at the same time we had not lost any players from the club, which was fantastic. It was great to see many lads still playing and not have the ridiculous 'rivalry' with United. For once there were no distractions and we were, at least for a few weeks in the summer, a football utopia, building a great team spirit and watching the World Cup together; it was great fun.

The new second team was doing well. The guys who had stepped up to manage them were great and both teams got together socially as one big group on several occasions; it felt like a proper club and we were all happy campers. Then disaster struck. It was very obvious that as a team that had only just avoided relegation the season before, we needed to go into the same division again. It was also very obvious that our new second team needed to go in the division below. They were brand-new, quite inexperienced; it was very clear and, more to the point, that was supposed to be the policy. But some things never change and the league had their AGM and certain clubs with representatives on the league were allowed to go to whatever division they wanted whilst we were told that my team had to go to the division above (Division 1, just below premiership), even though we had come two points off the bottom of Division 2 and the year before had been in Division 6. Similarly, our second team had been put in Division 2 (where my team should have been), which they were not ready for at all. It was unfair on both counts and I knew immediately would ruin the season.

I thought we were good enough to do OK in the higher division with all the changes, but it was not the point. There were meant to be rules and sportsmanship within the league. It should not have been possible for some clubs to choose where they went. I had seen it happen for years where teams deliberately went into a lower division in order to win it and I had heard horror stories of other teams folding as a result. My younger son had played an entire season for his team one year because the 'team officer' dealing with the league had made a mistake on the form. They found themselves in a division too high and lost every single game; it was miserable. Integrity and sportsmanship are crucial when it comes to teams and divisions; it literally will be the difference between a child enjoying or hating his football if his team is playing at completely the wrong standard. In any season and division, as the season develops, you will get whipping boys and weaker teams emerge, but double-figure wins should not be happening much in a league game against a team from the same division.

Our second team was so new and inexperienced, consisting mainly of players who had played for us or United the previous season who had come near the bottom and rock bottom respectively. In all good conscience, no league should ever have made that decision. To really kick us in the teeth, every other club around us, often with more teams than us, got the division they requested every time. They were much bigger than us and they had club officials also working in the league, and seemingly our club had very little 'influence'.

I immediately kicked up a fuss, expecting the club's full backing, I repeatedly presented the league with positions, the results of all the teams involved and proof that the wrong teams had been put in the divisions we should have been in. Probably the most insulting, ridiculous explanation given was that 'there were no vacancies' in our correct divisions, which was meaningless; it would have been more polite to say 'piss off', as it was their choice to put other teams in these divisions, causing there to be no vacancies.

The club was clueless; they just did not have any influence with the league at all. This had happened previously to their teams and had ended very badly, with teams folding, yet they still were unable to change anything. At one point I met with the club secretary, who told me he would 'sort it out' and speak to one of his contacts at the county FA who had some influence and who would deal with the league. Sadly his 'sorting it out' consisted of a single email to a bureaucrat at Essex FA, who I think did actually tell him to piss off. His email after this summed it up, sent to me and my assistant/ coach: "*Simon and ____ you know i know it's not fair as iv been there, i have tried to take the league on but one club is just not enough.*"

Not being quite as ready to lay down, I contacted the FA directly and put my concerns to them. I was not going to be fobbed off; I had too many kids' welfare at stake. This time, after copying every name I could find on their website to my email, I got a reply saying there was an appeals process to decisions like this and I needed to complete the appeals form. This was crazy, as our league had told the club repeatedly there was no appeals process, and the decision was final; the club official dealing with the league knew nothing about this despite doing the role for over a decade. Ironically, the email was from the guy who had blanked our club secretary a couple of weeks previously. I immediately questioned him as to why he had kept this appeals process quiet to my club for the last decade or more (which could have saved several other teams from folding in the past and kids could still be playing), which was completely ignored.

I immediately completed the form and provided all the background evidence and information. This awful man came back a few days later to tell me that the appeal had to be made within fourteen days of the decision, which we had passed. I argued that the fourteen days had to start from when we became aware because it had been hidden from my club for ten years or more. You guessed it, they refused to allow me to appeal, as fourteen days had expired since the divisions were set, even though they had deliberately not disclosed the process even existed until after fourteen days and some pressure from me. I was disgusted; the sheer manipulation and deceit involved was something I had never seen, and this was all to make sure preferred teams in a junior league got to play where they wanted. Where was the fairness or integrity? It was so wrong and set such terrible examples to the children who naïvely expected more from adults in authority.

In the meantime, rather than thank me for finding out about this appeals process which could help many teams and boys in the future, something they had not been able to identify in ten years or more, the club was now pissed off with me for kicking up a fuss and upsetting the league – *they* somehow were upset! I offered to help the club and to work with them and against the league to ensure this did not happen again, which would protect future teams, but I was apparently 'rocking the boat' with the league and needed to accept it for both the teams. I had not always agreed with everything the club did, but I thought they were well intentioned. This was different: for them to turn a blind eye to obvious corruption worried me, especially as they had been very keen on our second team joining. Now the boys were all signed up and had paid subs they did not want to know; I never thought I would see this side to them.

I could not be bothered arguing anymore, it was pointless even raising a concern, and I knew it was only for one last season, but at the same time a season is a long time. My guardian angel came in the unlikely form of the manager and chairman of another local club who could not fill in all of his registered teams. They were a bigger club, had lots of pitches we were allowed to use (we still were not allowed to use our own pitch in preseason) and one of the teams they needed to fill was in our correct division. It took all of three seconds to realise it made perfect sense to take the team and switch clubs; it was perfect.

The team met the following day and, aside from a couple of concerns and objections which we discussed, the whole squad and parents were happy to leave; it was a no-brainer in fairness. Parents even saved money. The only resistance was my assistant, who was desperate to stay as he had applied to be an 'officer' for the club and was worried it would jeopardise his chances (which was ridiculous – they would take anyone who volunteered). We took a vote of the players and with a 15-1 landslide majority it was agreed. I sent an email to the chairman, copying in the officers that night.

The next morning was total carnage; for a team that no one had been remotely interested in helping at any point in weeks, suddenly we were in demand. I had not had a single call or email from the chairman to this point. However, the prospect of losing sixteen lots of subs finally prompted a reaction. By 6am I was told that he 'understood my frustrations' and that he felt 'the league could step in' and to wait to hear from him later that day. Wow, I should have just threatened to leave from the start! The guy had ignored me for a year!

I then got a call from my mate the club officer, telling me that he'd heard all about the meeting at training the previous night and the vote to leave from my assistant, who called him in tears late at night begging for the club to do something as he did not want to leave the club. It was all very strange; I did not know what to believe. I did not want anyone to get upset or cause any problems, but I had to put my team first. The email I received that morning was the email I wanted when it had all happened. To cut a very long story short, a deal was done between City, our new club and the league, whereby City effectively took the new club's space they could not fill. The chairman of the club we were going to join was an absolute gentleman, the one guy who also wanted to put the kids first. He could have been uncooperative with City and gained a team.

Personally, I still wanted to leave: too much had happened, and I was very uneasy about the fact that we had been ignored by the chairman, who had been aware of the irregularities with the league for weeks but within a day had sorted out a deal when he thought we were leaving and that he was going to be losing money. But I did not want to offend anyone, and if it meant that much to my assistant, I could live with staying. I did not really care which club we were under; it was our team. The colours we played in did not really matter to me, the players or the parents. We agreed that as long as he dealt with the club and I just focused on the team, I would see it out with City for the last season.

What a bad decision that was. They were not going to forgive and forget anytime soon. I had gone against them and the league; it did not matter that I was right, and we should be questioning misconduct within the league. I had questioned their authority and 'upset the league'; this was not the done thing. It was much better to talk a good game, complaining about how bad the leagues were at our monthly meetings, but do nothing at all whenever a real issue arose. I was gutted; I had really liked the club and the people, but they could not get past the team wanting to leave or me questioning anything. They saw it as a personal attack and insult; it really was not anything like that. I saw it as a good thing that we had identified an appeals process which could help future teams put in the wrong divisions. Many teams within the club had folded in the past and some kids had never played again; this process could have avoided that. I did not expect thanks, but I certainly did not expect hostility for doing something that could benefit the club and future players.

We played some friendlies and started training in late August. I could not have been happier with how the squad was coming together: the new players improved the squad but also gelled with the existing lads. Just as importantly, the parents were a breath of fresh air, supportive and respectful – I had never had it so good.

One of the games almost descended into chaos due to parents again. It was a brilliant game in midweek; both teams were great and we won it 1-0. Before the game we had agreed to make it thirty minutes each half as it was still summer and sweltering. The referee, who was one of their parents, decided to make it thirty-five minutes both halves as we scored early and they needed a goal! I could not believe it when the second half went on nearly forty minutes and that was after speaking to him at half time to make sure he knew it was thirty minutes a half. In the last minute, one of our boys was late in a tackle and their team and parents erupted, demanding he was sent off. The match should have finished ten minutes previously! Another example of parents setting all the wrong examples when it comes to sportsmanship, even in a friendly having the whole 'win at all costs' mentality.

Our first game of the season was against our second team; it was not an ideal game to start with. We wanted them to do well but at the same time wanted to try and challenge for the league. There was loads of banter amongst the players at school in the week before, as you would expect. The second team had played the week before and had played very well and were unlucky to only draw in their first league game. I woke up on Sunday morning and I have never seen weather like it in September. It was freezing cold and pouring with rain and windy, even though it had been sunny all week. We conceded within a minute, which was not the start to the season I was hoping for, but we settled down and managed to turn it round in a game that could well have been called off, it was so cold and wet.

The week after we played a team from a nearby town; they had been in the division above the year before, so we knew it would be hard. It was a horrible game mainly due to the constant aggression and abuse from their parents and manager. Every single decision was met by screaming and shouting, claiming for handballs, fouls, free kicks, offsides, throw-ons – it was so tedious. At one point their manager marched onto the pitch to have a hissy fit and scream further at the referee. We won 1-0 but my main memory about that day was texting the referee later that day and asking if he was OK and that I would happily make a complaint against the manager's conduct, and his reply was, "Don't worry, I have had worse." Aside from actual physical violence, I am not sure what could be worse than what I had witnessed. The poor lad was not much older than my players.

Our next game was a County Cup match against a premiership team from our own league. The County Cup is an interesting cup, as you can end up playing any team in the county at all levels. So you could get a team in the bottom division of our local league playing against an EJA team from a different league; it was not uncommon to see 10-0 or even 15-0 in this competition. This game was wonderful, everything good about football, which was nice after the previous week.

It was lovely to see the boys really give it a go against a premiership team; we really did match them and you could almost see the team building and confidence flowing in front of you. We went 1-0 down early on and it looked like it was going to stay that way when we missed a couple of chances in the second half. In the last two minutes we got a free kick, halfway between the corner flag and the penalty area. One of the lads on the bench at the time suggested we get our big (newly converted) winger, who I had taken off at half time, up for the cross. I took his advice and sent the lad on. Our captain delivered the perfect cross which, you guessed it, was met by the super sub with a looping header which stayed in the air for what seemed like an hour before nestling into the top corner. What a sub, what a goal – the boys went mad. We were back in this game. 1-1 at full time, 1-1 after extra time – the dreaded penalty kicks. We missed our first one, they scored, we scored, they missed, we both scored our next two.

We scored our fifth and our keeper pulled off a great save to save their fifth and we had done it.

That was the point when we really started to look like a team, and more crucially it was the day that the boys gained so much confidence and belief in themselves and realised that if you are a team, anything is possible. The other team's manager was a gentleman; he was very complimentary about us, and the referee was brilliant and complimented both teams on their conduct and the spirit in which the game had been played. I passed on the positive feedback to the club, as I thought it reflected very well on the boys which was of course ignored.

Every game from thereon in was brilliant: confidence was so high and everyone was loving it. The boys never missed a single training session, parents were brilliant, friendships were formed with both the players and parents. The mix of players was brilliant; it was amazing seeing these guys improve so much from the season before. As ever, though, you are only ever one game away from more chaos and violence.

We then played a premiership team for the first time in the league cup, which was a massive test. I should not have worried. We were sensational: went 2-0 up, they then scored in second half to make it 2-1, but we scored a header from a corner straight after and then in the last minute we made it 4-1, sparking wild celebrations from the whole bench and me. I thought we could do well, but this was beyond my wildest dreams. We had improved so quickly; this really could be our season.

The uneasy relationship with the club took a turn for the worse soon after, when we had had our first injuries of the season. Our goalkeeper's leg was pitch black, the bruising was so bad from some muscle damage; our skipper had a bad back, along with two or three other players with various knocks and a couple who were unavailable. Luck was very much on our side: our next game was the third-round County Cup match, which was the one competition that did not really matter as the best EJA teams from across the county were in it, and for local league teams it was more a training exercise and an opportunity to play different teams. The two games we had played had been great fun, but with so many matches to fit in still and there being the two cups still, we had to put the boys' safety first. Plus make sure they were OK to play in the game the week after that really was big in the League Cup.

We left it as late as possible but come the Saturday morning we had no choice and I emailed the club secretary to let him know we were going to have to cancel the game; I had taken advice from a friend at the league who had agreed it was the right call and correct to put the boys first. However, by this point the club was gunning for us, anything they could find to cause problems, and this was another opportunity.

This time I was told I had taken away the boys' opportunity to play football! You could not make it up: we had played every week since early August; we had won every game. The boys were loving it and again we were being told we should play a game with injured players, just so we didn't incur a fine and upset the league.

I felt very strongly about the situation; I was not going to put my players' wellbeing at risk, especially when we had a massive cup game the following week, which was something we could do well in. Kids will always want to play. I understood playing football was important but not to the point of damaging players' health, which is where adults need to be adults and put their welfare first. I even offered to step down if any parent or player was not happy with what I was trying to do, but as ever it was only them. Thankfully common sense prevailed, and everyone agreed to stay united and not let the club or league cause problems again. I was, however, told I had to pay the £50 fine for not being able to field a team by the club. By this point I decided I would rather pay it than have another tedious argument.

My decision to not risk playing injured players in the County Cup match was very much vindicated the following week in a hellish game against the same team who had caused all sorts of unpleasantness in the league game between their manager and parents. This time they were at home, and it was even worse. We very much needed every player fit to play; it was a nightmare. More tantrums from the manager, their parents screaming to their players to 'take him out' in reference to our players, a referee barely older than the players being terrorised into making bad decision after bad decision (even after I had begged the league to provide a strong older referee this time). Somehow, we won, and the best part of the day was coming home.

We won the next couple of games as well, which were largely uneventful aside from, in one of them, a parent coming over to the managers' side close to us and his own manager to repeatedly scream in reference to my team that 'they don't want it, they are rattled'. He should not have been there but looked a nuisance; there was only five minutes left, so we ignored him. It made no sense in any event; we must have wanted it a little bit – we were winning 3-0!

We kept winning until the new year, getting better every game. The confidence was growing, and off the pitch parents and players were all getting on so well. We played a game just before Christmas, again a team with the smallest pitch we had played on in years; it was really weird. And it seemed to get to the players: the first half was terrible, we were lucky to go in at half time at 1-1, and there were a few arguments and some unrest. It was not like us at all. In the second half we settled down and played some great stuff, winning 4-1, and went into Christmas unbeaten. At that point, for the first time I was convinced we could win something. My personal highlight was my son scoring the fourth goal and sealing the win, and the wild celebrations and bundles that followed right in front of me. I may have even gone on the pitch to celebrate with them, which I should not have done!

Things were getting so exciting: we were top of the league and in the quarter-finals of both cups. Where was this season going to take us? I was, however, very worried for the second team; they had started off brightly with a draw but had lost every game since and had started losing heavily. They were simply in the wrong division. As a new team they could not be expected to be competitive against established teams that had been together for years. The club and league had really let those boys down. Even worse, they had been involved in an abandoned match; it sounded horrendous: allegations of players being assaulted, parents, including mums, being threatened.

In January, the inevitable happened and our second team folded. It had been a miserable and completely predictable experience. I had warned the club time and time again that they needed to help them and raise a complaint to the league. At that age, no one is going to turn up every week to get smashed. I was gutted, as I knew most of the lads; some had played for me in previous seasons, and it was my idea to have a second team, so I felt partly responsible.

Of course, no apology from the league or club, and the club did not even refund half a season's subs which was meant to be towards referees and pitches, both of which would not now be needed for the remaining games. Some of the boys never played again. The club was fine; they had received £2k from the team, half of which was not used. The league was OK; they received their fees. Not so great for the manager, his assistant and all the players and parents. I was so disappointed in the club; I had given them the benefit of the doubt for a long time and tried to understand their animosity to me and maintained they were good people with different views on junior football. But this was a hard one to take; it was wrong on every level right from the start. The team had been effectively set up to fail.

Desperate to return to football, we had to wait as the weather was awful. We finally played again in late January against a team near the bottom. We won the game, but it should not have really been played, it was so muddy; the boys could not stand up, let alone run or pass. There were two memorable incidents. One was where one of their players went in for a tackle and end up tripping and going headfirst into the mud. It was really nasty because the mud had literally covered him and gone into one eye; the lad had to come off. Then in the last couple of minutes of the game, our winger, who was a lovely kid but probably our most temperamental player, got fouled quite badly right in front of me and the other manager. Inexplicably he lashed out in retaliation, literally kicking the other player with the ball long gone. In all honesty he should have been sent off; it was stupid, and he deserved a red card, but the referee was lenient, as it was the last minute, and he gave a yellow.

I immediately substituted him, and the final whistle went soon after. But their managers and a parent went mad at the referee, accusing him of cheating and being on our side. I was honest and said I would have had no complaints if the boys had been sent off, but the referee had been excellent the whole game and it was a contentious decision. I had always got on well with their manager going back years, so I text him later to see how his lad who had hurt his eye was and said again I would have had no issue if my lad had been sent off. But he ignored me completely and then did not end up playing the return match later in the season. I wasn't sure what I had done wrong but thought it was a bit childish, especially when I remembered back to when we had won the bottom division and him saying he had brought his team down a division to win it at the start of the year. Bit rich now to be all about sportsmanship.

After an absolute battle in Basildon against our close rivals in one cup we finally got past them after extra time with two late goals. Our keeper kept us in the cup with an amazing save in the last minute of normal time. And then, for the first time ever, we played a team in the division below us in the semi-final, who had gone unbeaten all season and was better than many of the teams in our division. We did enough to get through: a goal in each half, winning 2-0. We were in a cup final; this was after one cup win in the previous five years! This was the one I wanted. I knew we had a chance at the start of the season, and it would be at a proper ground under floodlights, evening kick-off – the boys were going to love it.

The League Cup, which we were well and truly outsiders for, was a bonus, but we were so confident and strong by now, I knew they could give anyone a game. And in the quarter-final and semi-final I saw the greatest performances I have ever seen; it was truly like watching Brazil! In the quarter-final we were away against a team in the division above us, I thought it would be close as I knew we were now more than at that level, but it was easy. We were outstanding; I have never seen such brilliant performances from wingers, they were amazing, and the crossing was fantastic and strikers brilliant again. We won 6-1 – it was their biggest loss of the season; their manager afterwards said we were the best team they had played. I was so proud of the team, and I thanked all the parents and players for their support. We were now in the semi-final of the big one, the League Cup, and were one game from Roots Hall the home of Southend United, a professional team. The only obstacle was the small matter of the premiership leaders and cup holders, who we had to play in the semi-finals.

That day in Southend in March will be remembered by every player and parent involved; it was magical. It had brilliant football, superhuman commitment, high drama, huge emotion – it was like a movie. This stuff does not happen in real life, but it did that day. By this time the team was full of confidence; we were in one final, on course to win the league, and the boys felt unstoppable. I knew that it would take a superhuman effort to get past this team; the bottom line was that they had sixteen players who had played in the top division for years, so they were quality. We had three boys who had regularly played at that level and all the others had pretty much never played higher than the third division we were in now. We'd been in the sixth division only two seasons previously; we had no right whatsoever to win the game.

But I also knew that the team spirit we had was more powerful than any individual player and that the boys wanted this so badly. They were used to winning now, confidence was so high and they really fancied it. All of these factors made for a very powerful advantage. I was more excited than the kids, I think. I am not sure I believe in destiny, but the night before I decided on the team and formation and remember saying to my long-suffering wife that we would nick it.

Even the parents, who had been fantastic all season, had their doubts that morning; one of them said to me he just wanted us to give them a good game and it not be a cricket score. My expectations were much higher, and that day I felt like Pep, Clough, Ferguson and José all rolled into one. The pre-match talk was great; the lads were so pumped. I made it clear that they deserved to be here and were on this level now – we were ready. By the time the whistle went to start the game, they were ready to go to a war, let alone a football match, and best of all they followed the tactics and game plan to a tee. My plan was not particularly sophisticated: it went something along the lines of coming out like men possessed, put them under pressure early, go long in first few minutes, put defenders under pressure and hopefully get an early goal or two, and then hopefully, as it slowed down, keep the ball a bit and defend for your lives.

For the first twenty minutes our opponents did not know what had hit them: our boys were like men possessed and more. I have never seen energy and commitment like it. From keeper to striker, every tackle, every header, every second ball, we were first, and the passing was sensational. And best of all, the going long early worked. After five minutes our keeper launched the ball into orbit; it went miles and bounced not far from their area. Our striker was on his toes already and broke free of one centre back. The ball bounced into their penalty area, the keeper hesitated, the other centre back was running with our man. Brave as you like, our man got to the ball first before the keeper and defender, and headed it into the net, taking a whack in the process. Players and parents erupted; it was so early in the game, but what a start. We were excellent all half; agonisingly we hit the post from a header ten minutes after the goal. At half time we were looking good, but there was no way we could carry on at that pace.

The next forty-five minutes were the longest of my life; they started coming into the game much more and we were getting deeper and deeper. We took off a striker who had been quality to add another man in midfield and left the goal-scorer upfront on his own; he must have run a marathon that day. With twenty minutes to go, I started thinking it could happen. They then missed a big chance, and I was certain it was only a matter of time before they equalised. With ten minutes to go our midfielder hit a beautiful twenty-five yarder with his left foot; it was in all the way but hit the inside of the post (again) and did not go over the line, and I was certain they would go to the other end and get a lucky goal.

The last ten minutes were horrific; I felt physically sick. We were so close and the boys deserved this so much. All game plans were out the window. It was just defend for dear life and smash the ball as far away as possible. Minute by minute, the clock was moving towards full time; they were getting closer – could we hold out for just a few minutes more? Time was up, we screamed/pleaded/begged the referee to end our misery. He announced there would be four minutes of injury time. My heart sank; I have never seen so much injury time in a junior football match.

A few more minutes elapsed and I seriously did not feel well; our keeper then did one of the greatest goal kicks I have ever seen (even better than his assist for the goal). He managed to hit it over the halfway line but off the pitch, the ball bouncing away for miles, not for the first time that season – our keeper, what a legend. My parents, funnily enough, didn't run to get it – another minute gone. Our opponents were now complaining about time-wasting (forgetting they'd had four minutes' injury time already). Finally, mercifully, the referee blew that whistle – we had done it: we were going to play at Roots Hall, and we'd knocked out the holders and we deserved it. The last ten minutes were rugged, but over the course of the game we were the better team – hit the woodwork twice; it could have been two or three. What was also very satisfying was that the referee and linesman were very complimentary again about the way we'd played and conducted ourselves, and our parents were sensational. I could hear them all game cheering the boys on – all so positive. It was the perfect game; I was very so proud of everyone involved.

Madness ensued – hugs, tears, joy – it was wonderful and everything that is good about our beautiful game. I don't know what I said after the game apart from that I was the proudest football manager in the world and that I knew we would do it. My wife could confirm that I had even put some bubbly in my boot that night to prove it; I just had a feeling we could do it. Unfortunately, our opponents had not left yet so I thought it might be rubbing it in to start cracking open a bottle of bubbly. We certainly made up for it later: I invited everyone to the social club thinking a few would come, but every single parent and player made it. That day was more than football; it was about the team and togetherness. I was on cloud nine being part of this amazing team and knowing my son and his mates were having the time of their lives.

The club, through gritted teeth, had to offer their congratulations on social media. For a manager and team that did it all the 'wrong' way, it was perplexing to say the least to have so many happy players and parents, not to mention the small matter of two cup finals and a possible league title. One of my parents asked a few days after the semi-final if the club would lay on a coach for the boys and parents for the finals. I think I laughed at him, but I said I would get my assistant to ask them. To my amazement they agreed to do it; on reflection it was a huge PR exercise. We were the most successful team they had probably ever had; locally getting to the cup finals was quite big, so they had no real choice.

Despite the fairly obvious intentions in making the offer, I tried to offer them an olive branch on behalf of the parents and me. I emailed the chairman and secretary thanking them and asking if we could agree to draw a line under what had happened and let bygones be bygones. Any doubts I had that their gesture was genuine were extinguished when they ignored me completely. Whilst publicly congratulating me and the boys, they did not even give me the courtesy of a response. It would have been better if they had said nothing and at least be true to their beliefs, but these guys did not have a genuine bone in their body.

After discussing with the parents and team we decided to take their money to pay for the coaches. Part of me wanted to decline and do it ourselves, but they had taken plenty from us, so we decided to take a little something back. We had played so many games by now; with preseason as well it was almost a year's solid football, and with GCSEs coming up, I would have liked the league to be over, but with the cup games there were still a few to play.

We played against our rivals to win the league; we knew if we won it would be the title, but it all went a bit wrong. I knew we were not right that day: the boys were messing around a bit, and we had to move grounds because their pitch was not marked out! We could have refused and taken the points, as kick-off was a set time and we kicked off about an hour later, but that was not us. We did not play well but took the lead in the first half; their striker then ran riot, tearing our defence apart and scoring two goals. Second half we had chances but looked a bit weary, and it finished 1-2. We were now in a bit of trouble because we still had to play them and another really tough team the week after.

We looked really out of salts in the next game and got well beaten 3-1 in Basildon; this was now a nightmare. We had gone all season without losing and lost two games in two weeks and could easily end up runners-up in three competitions. This was not the plan at all. Our luck had deserted us; we hit the post and bar a dozen times in the last few games. We had one more chance: the home game against our rivals for the league. This time we were up for it: started well, much more like we had been a few weeks previously. Finally, we had some luck with the woodwork; our skipper hit a long shot, it hit the bar yet again, but this time went back in off the keeper. It was what we needed desperately; you could see the weight lifted. The boys relaxed and played some good stuff, winning 3-0. Usually this would have meant big celebrations, but it seemed a bit subdued as we had the first cup final four days later on the Thursday evening. If we could win that, it really would be party time. Most of the boys had never won anything aside from our division six title; they could finish the week with two trophies.

What a night we had in Great Wakering for the first final. Everything about the experience was wonderful. One of our dads had a mate with a double-decker bus we could use so had room for the families and friends of all the boys. It had been raining on and off all day but, as if by magic, the rain stopped just before kick-off. It was a nice ground with proper stands and changing rooms; Great Wakering made us feel so welcome. The parents were all able to go in the bar before the game whilst we were getting ready; many other football mates came down and even a couple of managers from other teams came to wish us well. The whole evening was just a different level to anything we had experienced; the boys were superstars for the night.

As for the game itself, we were playing a team from another nearby town who was decent; we had struggled to beat them in the league and, unlike us, they had been in our division for a few years. We were flying, so we fancied our chances, and I was desperate for the boys to get the double. We started off well and, with around ten minutes gone, our striker, the hero from the semi-final, got on the end of a through ball, just beat the keeper to it, colliding in the process, and scored a great goal. Everyone was celebrating when, a few seconds later, the referee disallowed the goal and, to add insult to injury, booked our striker for the collision and imaginary offence only he had seen. Clearly the league was not willing to move on from us challenging them.

A few minutes later my son was scythed down about five minutes after making the pass; we retained possession and the advantage was played. I fully expected a yellow card to be dished out when the ball went off, but no action was taken at all. I should not have been worried: the same striker scored from a similar chance five minutes later, but this time it was impossible to invent a reason to not give it. Inexplicably several of the club 'officers' had turned up (to hopefully watch us lose), the same guys who had done everything to cause problems for the team all season and let down our second team so badly. They had faces like wet weekends, especially when the boys' celebrations were literally in front of them.

Shortly after, our other striker finished brilliantly to make it 2-0 at half time and their night was well and truly ruined.

At half time, I told the lad with yellow card to not make another tackle and pull out of any fifty-fifties to make it impossible for the referee to book him. One minute into the second half he scored again, and we never looked back. Our other striker scored another three goals; he was so clinical. We ran riot, winning 6-0. Nothing was going to stop us that night; every player in the squad had been brilliant.

The celebrations getting the trophy and in the changing room will never be forgotten; being under the floodlights made it more special. 'Sweet Caroline' blasting out, boys singing and laughing – they had won the double and most of the team had been playing in the sixth division only two seasons previously. Being in cup finals was something other teams did. The parents were all in the bar by the time we came out and again it was lovely; every boy was cheered as he came in. Very sensibly, the club officers had slunk off at the final whistle; I think they would have been lynched if they had set foot in the bar. I would have been at the front of the queue; this was the boys' and their parents' moment.

We had our last league game the following Saturday against the manager who had screamed (mostly abuse) continuously in the two games we already had played. I really did not want to play it; it was going to be grief again and I was worried that a lad could get injured or sent off and miss playing at Roots Hall. We came through it unscathed, though, winning 3-1 and ensuring we won the league by seven points (which sounded far more comfortable than it had been a couple of weeks previously). Despite it being a fairly meaningless game, the toys came well and truly out of the pram in the second half when our linesman missed a throw-in due to all of his subs sitting and standing on the touchline and blocking his view. When I explained our linesman (only a young lad) did not have X-ray vision and his players were meant to be well back from the touchline, he insisted we 'were fucking cheats'. It was a meaningless game: the season was over and still he could not help himself.

The big one at Roots Hall was underwhelming at best. Unlike Great Wakering, it was a lunchtime kick-off and there were other finals being played; I think they crammed four age groups in one day. It was rubbish: we had ten minutes to warm up (which is not long enough to even stretch and risks injury) and we were rushed in and out of the changing room and the pitch. If they had just reduced the day to three games being played it would have been better, but clearly it was just a case of getting the games played. At Great Wakering we had felt like superstars; at Roots Hall it was like being on a conveyor belt. The parents and support were brilliant again, but it was not the same; it seemed like the fantastic opportunity of playing at League One stadium had been spoilt by making it all so rushed.

We were playing a very good team near the top of the premiership, very similar to the team we had played in the semi-final. The boys were great again and gave everything they had; we had the same tactics as the semi-final and it almost worked: we started off well and hit the bar (for what seemed like the hundredth time that season), but we let in a soft goal just before half time and in the second half, in all honesty we were chasing shadows. Our opponents kept the ball very well and showed why they had been playing at a higher level for much longer than us. They deservedly won 3-0 and that was that: our season was over. If ever the cliché 'it was a game to many' was relevant, it was then. Two trophies and runners-up in the League Cup wasn't bad, though.

We went back to the social club again for an end-of-season drink and celebration of the season. It had been such an intense few weeks and the season had been so dramatic it was definitely time for a rest. The boys had their GCSEs, which they really needed to focus on; the season had gone on a long time with all the matches we played. Although we did have Holland still to come after they had done their exams. It was my last game, so I thanked all the lads and parents for being brilliant all year, and I was done: my junior football managerial career was over.

We all knew the team spirit created had been the main reason for the success and so much of that was due to playing games all the time, fun training, having social events and generally becoming a unit on and off the pitch. We were so lucky that it was one of those rare occasions that everyone mixed so well, and the parents wanted the same for the boys. There were a couple of exceptions, but with some parents you cannot win. If they could not get behind the manager and the team in a year like that, they really are not worth worrying about. It had been the greatest season any of us had ever had.

SC

AFTERMATH

Leaving junior football can be a hard decision to make, but as long as the kids are not being let down and everything is in place for the team to carry on, it shouldn't be. Having been away from managing, coaching and the politics of football for over four years now, I look back and wonder how I fitted everything in. My personal life seemed a lot busier back then as well. But after having left I could see that I was part of the problem sometimes! Football consumes you and you can easily get caught up in the so-called passion of it all, which I know I did on more than one occasion.

When I did step down from being a manager it was like a weight had been lifted off my shoulders and had given me a clearer view of what is wrong and what is good with junior football. Looking in from the outside you can see how wrong it can actually be. Watching a child walk over to his parents with a smile on their face only to be greeted with a furious-looking parent and be ushered straight to the car because the parent wasn't happy with something about the match. Not the child, the parent who wasn't playing! This probably happens at every game on a Sunday morning and there are many parents who, in the same situation, would put an arm around them and pick out all the good things they had done during the match. That is what should be happening across the board for all children. As a manager, I never really noticed things like this, as I was too busy gathering up the equipment or taking nets down, but as a parent it's something I did notice.

Apart from missing the actual coaching and the progression of the kids on and off the pitch, I can honestly say I don't miss all the other crap that comes with running a team. This is not to say that I wouldn't like to do it again knowing what I know now, but I would do it very differently. I wouldn't get so engrossed with it all where it takes over large parts of your life. I would teach football and that would pretty much be it; the politics I would leave to other people to deal with. I wouldn't get involved in any personal stuff, although that is hard as you do become attached to the kids and want only what is best for them. My advice to anyone considering junior football management would be that if you love football, have patience, can and want to invest your spare time, then do it, as there is much to be gained; from a personal point of view it can be very rewarding. I loved most of the football years and have some great memories, and I would never want to put anyone off from giving it a go.

However, I do hope this book could be a wakeup call to everyone involved in junior football as to the things happening week in, week out which ruin the game for the children and for us all. I hope that improvements can finally be made to make it an even safer and happier environment for our kids to play football in and enjoy themselves without any pressure. The referees shouldn't feel threatened or come under constant abuse; you can see why numbers are slipping away and people don't carry it on, as it can be more hassle than it's worth. Less children are playing football and far fewer are carrying on after junior level; it is hardly surprising when you consider how they were treated for most of their junior football careers by the adults. Football is massive, whether it be watching on TV, playing FIFA or actually going to watch a Premier League match. The best thing of all should be playing the game; it's an amazing sport to be a part of if adults are not spoiling it.

My last season watching my son wasn't the most enjoyable season as at under-eighteens it seems most young men are there to try and prove how hard they are rather than play football, and on many occasions, it spilled over into shoving and pushing. I understand this is part of growing up, but I bet if you put half of these so-called hard men in a boxing ring they would shit their pants, but while they feel safe to have another ten players on the pitch and a referee to try to stop any action, it will always carry on. I have been in changing rooms where the violence has been spoken about more than the football, which is very strange as football is supposedly a non-violent sport. It would be interesting to know if other sports talk about violence more than the actual sport they are playing.

I don't miss the club meetings and politics surrounding football either; I always used to say I could go and live on another planet without any knowledge of time then come back to a club meeting and I could tell you exactly what month we were in. They were so repetitive, year in, year out, and things never really changed. A few new faces would come and some old faces go, some thinking they could change the club for the better (myself included in that at one point). But you can't, as most committee members are hand-picked to support the chairman in his way of thinking – 'yes men', as we say. If you voiced a strong opinion on anything you would have three or four people fighting against you, telling you why it couldn't work. Had they tried it? No, so how did they know it wouldn't make the club better or be better for the kids! Unfortunately, things don't change at all; clubs will always talk a good game.

Having said all of this, it was still a great part of my life that I am grateful for. I still love the sport; I miss watching my son play and getting better at something he loved doing alongside his friends. The social events, the friendships made, the friendships lost, the winning of games, winning trophies, even the losing of cup finals all played a part and made me and the kids who we are today. So, invest what time you can and make sure if you give this sport a go that you are doing it for the right reasons – not to massage your own ego but to put smiles on the kids' faces who want to take part.

MJ

It had always been the plan for me to call it a day at the end of the under-sixteen season. At seventeen and eighteen it didn't really seem like junior football anymore; it was more like adult football, with more aggression and aggravation than ever. The boys had done so well: they were all ready to play in the premier division of our local league; we had beaten two of the top four in the premiership, so they were more than ready to play at that level. Two or three players did really well and left to play for teams in the Eastern Junior Alliance, which was great to see. Towards the end of the season, I had asked Mark if he wanted to come out of junior football retirement and manage the team in the next season, but he was sensibly enjoying his time away from it all. At one point it looked like the team would not continue, but eventually my assistant offered to do it.

The first thing he said was, "I am not looking to win anything or take it seriously." I think he had read a script prepared by the club. I had no issue at all in these sentiments, but I knew the players: they did want to win games and did take it seriously. It seemed the club was again pushing this ethos without even asking the players if they agreed. I don't think any team full of seventeen- and eighteen-year-olds is not interested in winning! I knew our guys very much wanted to win some more cups and play in the premiership.

My concerns were not unfounded when the club/new manager did not let the team apply to go in the premiership division, which the lads all deserved and I am sure would have done very well in. They were also not entered into the County Cup, which was quite ironic when I been accused of not giving players the opportunity to play in this competition when we could not fulfil a fixture the previous season. We had at least entered it and won a couple of games. They went into the second division, which bizarrely only had six teams, so the season consisted of only ten games. With only one or two friendlies arranged preseason, there were hardly any matches. They were far too good for the division and would have smashed it; they were still brilliant. Unfortunately, they got knocked out of the remaining cups early, which was a shame, meaning even less games. None if it really mattered in the end as Covid brought the season to an abrupt end in March.

Although it wasn't my team anymore, it was very difficult to not have a big attachment. We had played so many games the season before and had so many social gatherings. The guys just loved playing; if there were no league games any weekends, we would play friendlies all the time, sometimes even on a Saturday and Sunday. By the time the season ended early in March, they had played twelve games in seven months; there was a clear month between some games. At the same stage the previous season we had played twenty-five matches. I just didn't get it; they were a brilliant team and the lads loved playing football. Everything from above seemed to just be about going through the motions, doing the bare minimum.

They carried on the following season as well and at least they got to play in the premiership. Neither the club nor manager had a choice this time: the whole league was down to two divisions, with most teams ending at under-sixteen or under-seventeen level and players going on to adult football. Again, there were only six teams in the division and Covid and further lockdowns blocked a huge chunk of the season. Outside of football, I see most of the lads around; my son is still good friends with a few and others became close family friends. They have all grown up into fantastic young adults and I am still good mates with several of the parents.

Sadly, my first club United was still up to its tricks, even years on from our issues with them. I really wanted to support my younger son in his football; he had missed out on so much of my time in the previous five years, so I wanted to be there for him. He wanted to play with his mates at United. I vaguely knew the manager and he agreed to let him come to training and he would be picking the squad for the coming season over the next few weeks. I was worried about going back, especially as the same chairman was still there, but it had been over three years and my son had nothing to do with our differences, so I assumed it would be OK.

Depressing, naïve and wrong again. Six weeks into training, no squad had been announced and they told me that the team probably wouldn't be carrying on as the manager's son was leaving to play at a higher level so they would not have a manager. They let us train for all those weeks when we could have found another team. I even offered to manage the team so they did not have to fold, which the manager was happy with, but then the charmer chairman intervened and blocked it and let the team fold rather than let me take it on. The ease at which someone in that position would treat children that badly to settle a personal score was thoroughly depressing.

He was at it again with one of my old parents I bumped into. He had been the manager of one of the young age groups at United. He was very upset as his parents had gone behind his back and all conspired to get rid of him and his son as they did not want him as manager. This had been done with the full knowledge and backing of the club and chairman. How horrible for the manager and, even worse, his son. Years later and they were still getting away with it.

We were now only a few weeks away from the season; I even frantically tried to start a team at another club, but it was all too late: all the teams were full, squads decided. Eventually my son found another team in a higher division which was very good. He did really well and would have been playing in a cup final until the dreaded Covid struck.

Nowadays I enjoy watching junior football; I still have mates managing teams and the best part is that I have no emotional involvement anymore. I can actually relax and enjoy the game. But now I am not emotionally involved I see things for what they are and realise that so much of what I (and every other junior football manager in the country) witnessed and experienced is not right, and we all have a collective responsibility to set a far better example to our children. Leagues, clubs, managers, coaches, parents, everyone needs to do more because it is not pretty out there and I am under no illusions that I was in a relatively tame league and area. There is probably far worse happening in some places.

Ultimately, despite all the absolute BS you contend with, I would not have changed a single thing of my experience. I made a million mistakes, didn't know what I was doing most of the time and hated 75% of the role, which mainly is adults doing their level best to ruin it for the kids. But kids were brilliant, and when you do play a part in giving them some positive experiences and creating great memories, you willingly take all the crap on the chin. I look back now at the friendships formed, the social side, the tours to Holland and all the laughs along the way very fondly. And the icing on the cake was that we improved so much and got to play in cup finals and win trophies. It was amazing, and my son and his mates have some wonderful memories to look back on – I know I have.

SC

We hope that this book has given a realistic insight into the world of junior football. Our experiences will be similar to thousands of other managers across the country. We all have shared the same up and downs, as well as difficulties and frustrations of dealing with parents, leagues and clubs. We have been brutally honest. It would be easy to go along with the narrative we all see from the FA and leagues, but the positive messages you see promoting equality, respect and sportsmanship is not what you actually see on a Sunday morning.

We have very much been part of the problem and completely understand how hypocritical it is to be critical of behaviours that we were sometimes guilty of in one way or another and a culture that we saw as normal. After all, it's football, and it was the same when we were growing up and playing junior football; not much has changed at all from generation to generation. It is because we were involved that we can recognise that it was wrong then and is wrong now. Hopefully we can help raise some awareness of these problems. Adults are still ruining the football experience for children. It must finally be time to break the cycle and to start making some genuine and meaningful changes.

MJ and SC

This book is printed on paper from sustainable sources managed under the Forest Stewardship Council (FSC) scheme.

It has been printed in the UK to reduce transportation miles and their impact upon the environment.

For every new title that Matador publishes, we plant a tree to offset CO_2, partnering with the More Trees scheme.

For more about how Matador offsets its environmental impact, see www.troubador.co.uk/about/